Introduction to
Data Communications
and LAN Technology

Introduction to Data Communications and LAN Technology

Ed da Silva
CEng, MIERE, MSc, PhD

BSP PROFESSIONAL BOOKS

OXFORD LONDON EDINBURGH

BOSTON MELBOURNE

First published in Great Britain by
Collins Professional and Technical Books 1986
Reprinted by BSP Professional Books 1988,
1989

British Library Cataloguing in Publication Data
Da Silva, Ed
Introduction to data communications and LAN
technology.
1. Computer networks
I. Title
004.6   TK5105.5

ISBN 0–632–02251–5

BSP Professional Books
A division of Blackwell Scientific
   Publications Ltd
Editorial Offices:
Osney Mead, Oxford OX2 OEL
   (Orders: Tel. 0865 240201)
8 John Street, London WC1N 2ES
23 Ainslie Place, Edinburgh EH3 6AJ
3 Cambridge Center, Suite 208, Cambridge,
   MA 02142, USA
107 Barry Street, Carlton, Victoria 3053,
   Australia

Set by Eta Services (Typesetters) Ltd
Beccles, Suffolk
Printed and bound in Great Britain by
Mackays of Chatham PLC, Chatham, Kent

Contents

Preface

This book on computer communications is intended for non-technically minded people. It assumes no previous technical knowledge of computer communication and no mathematical skills beyond the ability to add, subtract and multiply. Ease of reading is ensured by many illustrations and examples drawn from our daily lives. Explanations of systems are followed by case studies of actual equipment. The book may also be read in small doses and left when the reader is busy because a list of abbreviations (appendix A) and a glossary of terms (appendix B) are included in the appendices to remind the reader of the main terms used in the book.

Practical minded people, students and commercially minded managers will find the book interesting because explanations are given in a simple manner with everyday examples used as similes. They will find that the book explains in simple language the technical jargon used in computer communications. Understanding of these technical terms enables the reader to judge when he or she is being bluffed by technical terms to disguise imperfections in knowledge or equipment.

However, the book does not stop at basic explanations of technical terms. It establishes foundations and enables the reader to progress to a deeper understanding of data communication technology. It does this by providing a list of technical books (appendix E) for greater understanding, a list of selected papers and articles (appendix F) for practical systems and a list of the International Telegraph and Telephone Committee Interface recommendations – CCITT V Recommendations (appendix C) and CCITT X Recommendations (appendix D).

The book will be revised and updated as required and the author will be pleased to hear from readers who may wish to offer constructive criticisms.

Ed da Silva

CHAPTER 1
Communication Systems

1.1 INTRODUCTION

Computer communications techniques are based on the methods which we use in communicating with each other, and the purpose of this section is to introduce you to some of these methods. As you read on, you will probably be amazed to see the similarity between the techniques used by computers and those which we use in our daily lives but if you reflect for a while, you will cease to be surprised because computers are incapable of original thinking and can only follow what we program them to do.

Computer techniques may differ slightly. For example they use electrical signals instead of voice signals, and the speed of communication may differ but the main purpose of conveying information remains the same.

I will begin chapter 1 by using simple examples to show you what points we must consider in a communications system. I will then show you why we must consider these points and then go on to introduce the technical terms used so that you will be completely at ease when discussing these terms with computer experts. If you find this approach too elementary, please bear with me for a little while because I am only preparing the foundations for those not as knowledgeable as yourself.

1.2 BASIC ELEMENTS OF A COMMUNICATIONS SYSTEM

Let us start off by considering the simple case where you and I want to exchange messages. We will need the following:

(a) A *sender* – you to send the message.
(b) A *receiver* – me to receive your message.
(c) A *transmission medium* – to carry your message to me.
(d) *Addressing* – so that we know where to send your message.
(e) *Co-operation* – a form of protocol between you and me (sender and receiver), so that we know when to send and when to receive messages.

The above list illustrates some of the factors which we must consider in mess-

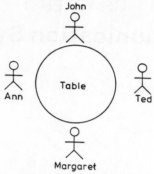

Fig. 1.1 After dinner conversation.

age transmission. It is by no means complete, because among other things, there is no assurance that the message sent

(f) is error free,
(g) is compatible with the transmission medium,
(h) is in a form which can be used by the receiver,
(i) has been successfully received.

Furthermore, I have considered message or data transferral in one direction only. What happens when communications is bi-directional? To analyse this, I will start off by choosing a very simple example. Consider the case (Fig. 1.1) where Ann, Margaret, Ted and John are having an after dinner conversation, and

(a) *Ann wants to speak to Ted*

The following ten points should be noted:

(1) *Sender* – Ann is the source of conversation.
(2) *Addressing* – Ann must address Ted to indicate that she wants to speak to him. This is necessary otherwise Margaret or John might think that Ann wants to speak to them.
(3) *Receiver* – Ted is the destination for the conversation.
(4) *Protocol (co-operation)* – Ann must arrange some protocol with Ted to decide when she should speak and he should listen. It is also important and good manners that Margaret and John observe the protocol and keep quiet whilst either of them is speaking.
(5) *Transmission code* – Ann must speak in a language which can convey a message to Ted. For example, it is useless for Ann to speak to Ted in English if Ted only understands French.
(6) *Transmission rate* – Ann must speak at a rate at which Ted can receive her message. Speaking too fast will result in garbled speech. Speaking too slowly will unnecessarily drag out the conversation and prevent others from speaking.

(7) *Transmission synchronisation* – Ann must speak only at times when Ted is listening. You should also note that Ann will communicate serially, i.e. she will complete one word before following it with another word. This process is called *serial transmission. Parallel transmission* is the case where all the words are spoken simultaneously. It is obviously not suitable for this particular occasion.

(8) *Transmission medium (interface)* – Ann must speak through a transmission medium (air) which will convey her message to Ted, speaking loudly enough (amplitude) so that Ted can hear her message.

(9) *Error detection and correction* – the ability to detect and correct any errors which may have happened during the conversation. Errors can occur due to pronunciation (source error) or speech loss due to a noisy aeroplane flying overhead (transmission error).

(10) *Transmission efficiency* – Ann must be able to convey what she wants to say to Ted in an efficient manner by choosing her words carefully to express her message.

Now consider the case, when

(b) *Ted replies to Ann*

When Ted replies to Ann, the same ten points mentioned in (*a*) apply.

The foregoing example should explain to you why the ten points mentioned above are often considered in any communications system. The communications systems in this book will be described in a similar manner but the descriptions will be biased towards the use of digital signals, the normal 'speech language' of computers.

I will therefore begin by defining some of the transmission terms which will be used. Try to understand them. Do not worry too much if you forget the abbreviations used in the description. A list of abbreviations is included in appendix A and a brief glossary of the terms is included in appendix B for your reference.

1.3 TRANSMISSION DEFINITIONS

A communications system can be one way (Figs 1.2 and 1.3). A one way only communications system is usually called a *simplex* system.

A communications system can allow communication in either direction

Fig. 1.2 A one way system.

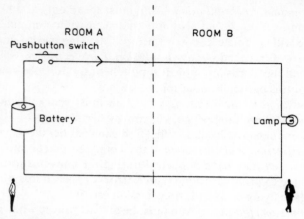

Fig. 1.3 A simple one way (simplex) communication system.

Fig. 1.4 An either-way (half duplex) system.

but only in one direction at a time (Figs 1.4 and 1.5). A communications system of this nature is called a *half duplex* system.

A system that allows communications in both directions simultaneously is called a *full duplex* communications system (see Figs 1.6 and 1.7).

1.4 TRANSMISSION CODES

In all cases of communication, the signals sent should convey a message to the receiver. For example, it is pointless speaking in English to people who do not understand English because they will not understand your message.

In addition to this, the message signals sent must reach the intended destination, i.e., the signals sent must be suitable for the transmission medium. For example, two astronauts on a space walk cannot speak directly to each other because voice signals (sound waves) cannot travel in an airless medium.

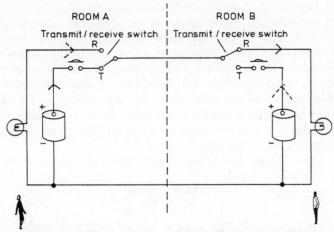

Fig. 1.5 Simple either way (half duplex) communication system.

Fig. 1.6 A both-way (full duplex) system.

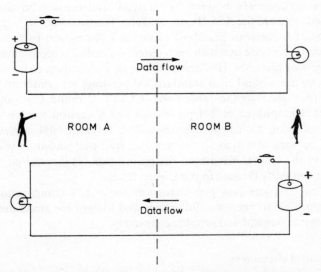

Fig. 1.7 A simple both-way (full duplex) communication system.

However, they can communicate with each other by using their voice signals to modify (modulate) a radio carrier wave which can traverse the airless medium. At the receiving end, the voice signals are removed (demodulated) from the radio wave carrier. The processes of converting and reconverting signals from one form to another without losing the information content of the signals are called *modulation* and *demodulation* respectively. A *modem* is a device which can carry out modulation and demodulation. Its name is an acronymn of MOdulation and DEModulation. In the case mentioned above, you should also note that the radio wave has acted as a *carrier* for the voice signals, therefore it is called the *carrier wave*.

An example of encoding and decoding is shown in Fig. 1.8. In this system,

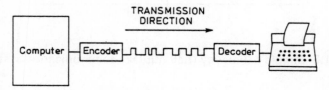

Fig. 1.8 Transmission encoding and decoding.

computer signals are encoded into electrical signals which are transmitted through wires to a decoder which reconverts the signals back into a form which operates the typewriter.

1.5   ASCII CODE

Many types of codes are used for digital signal transmission but the two most widely used ones are the ASCII code and the Baudot code.

The ASCII (American Standard Code for Information Interchange – see Fig. 1.9) code is a code in which each letter or symbol is represented by seven binary digits or bits. ASCII is one of the most widely used data transmission codes. There are a number of standardised versions with different names but basically they refer to the same code. CCITT (Comité Consultatif International Télégraphique et Téléphonique) has a version known as CCITT alphabet no. 5 or, as it is sometimes called, International Alphabet no. 5. National options are also sometimes incorporated within this code. For example, in the United Kingdom, the pound sign (£) is required, whereas it would not normally be used in the United States.

Seven information bits per character allow 128 combinations, which makes it possible to encode a full upper and lower case alphanumeric code with additional control and graphic characters.

1.5.1   Control characters

There are 32 control characters and these can be found in columns 0 and 1 of Fig. 1.9. These characters may be divided into four main categories:

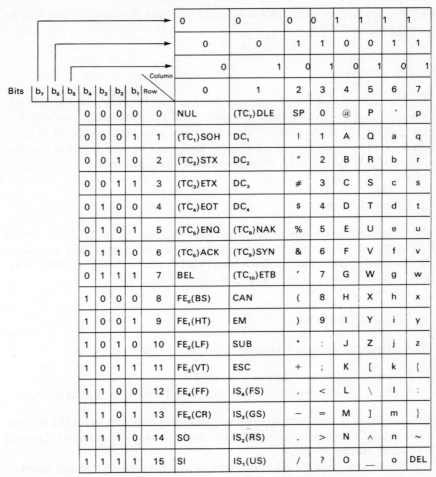

						Column	0	0	0	0	1	1	1	1
							0	0	1	1	0	0	1	1
							0	1	0	1	0	1	0	1
Bits b7	b6	b5	b4	b3	b2	b1 Row	0	1	2	3	4	5	6	7
0	0	0	0	0	NUL	(TC₇)DLE	SP	0	@	P	`	p
0	0	0	1	1	(TC₁)SOH	DC₁	!	1	A	Q	a	q
0	0	1	0	2	(TC₂)STX	DC₂	"	2	B	R	b	r
0	0	1	1	3	(TC₃)ETX	DC₃	#	3	C	S	c	s
0	1	0	0	4	(TC₄)EOT	DC₄	$	4	D	T	d	t
0	1	0	1	5	(TC₅)ENQ	(TC₈)NAK	%	5	E	U	e	u
0	1	1	0	6	(TC₆)ACK	(TC₉)SYN	&	6	F	V	f	v
0	1	1	1	7	BEL	(TC₁₀)ETB	'	7	G	W	g	w
1	0	0	0	8	FE₀(BS)	CAN	(	8	H	X	h	x
1	0	0	1	9	FE₁(HT)	EM	)	9	I	Y	i	y
1	0	1	0	10	FE₂(LF)	SUB	*	:	J	Z	j	z
1	0	1	1	11	FE₃(VT)	ESC	+	;	K	[	k	{
1	1	0	0	12	FE₄(FF)	IS₄(FS)	,	<	L	\	l	:
1	1	0	1	13	FE₅(CR)	IS₃(GS)	–	=	M	]	m	}
1	1	1	0	14	SO	IS₂(RS)	.	>	N	^	n	~
1	1	1	1	15	SI	IS₁(US)	/	?	O	_	o	DEL

Fig. 1.9 A version of CCITT No. 5 Code.

(a) Format effectors.
(b) Device controls.
(c) Information separators.
(d) Transmission controls.

(a) Format effectors

Format effectors are characters used to control the format of print; they conform approximately to the format keys (e.g. backspace, carriage return, etc.) of a typewriter. There are six format effectors, designated as FE_0–FE_5, and these can be found in column 0, rows 8–13 of Fig. 1.9. FE_0, corresponds to back space (BS), FE_1 to horizontal tabulation (HT), FE_2 to line feed (LF),

FE_3 to vertical tabulation (VT), FE_4 to form feed (FF) and finally FE_5 to carriage return (CR).

(b) Device controls

The four device control characters, designated DC_1–DC_4 in Fig. 1.9 are generally used to control switch on/switch off functions at a terminal. For example, DC_1 and DC_2 may be used to switch a cassette connected to a terminal on and off respectively. Similarly, DC_3 may be used to cause the contents of a VDU screen to be printed on an auxiliary printer.

(c) Information separators

The four information separators designated IS_1–IS_4 in Fig. 1.9 are available for delimiting records for easier handling by the computer. They are generally used in a hierarchical order where IS_1, IS_2, IS_3 and IS_4 are used to delimit units, records, groups and files of information.

(d) Transmission controls

Transmission control characters are used for two main purposes:

(1) to control the flow of data in a network
(2) to frame a message into an easily recognised format for the receiver.

Flow control is necessary to prevent messages being sent when the receiver is not ready. The sender may also want various forms of acknowledgement for its transmitted messages.

Message formats are used to minimise errors between sender and receiver. For example, a message might be too long to be sent all at one time, so it might be divided into five parts (see Figs 1.10 and 1.11). The first part, the header is preceded by the control character SOH to indicate that the information in the header might contain destination address, sending address, date, time, etc. This is then followed by the control character STX to indicate the start of the first block of text, ETB to indicate the end of the first block of text and so on.

A brief summary of the ten most important control characters is given in Fig. 1.11.

1.6   BAUDOT CODE

The Baudot code (Fig. 1.12) is named after a French engineer who worked on telegraphy around 1874. It is important because it is used on the Inter-

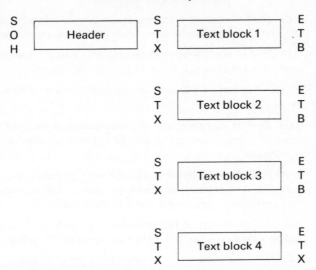

Fig. 1.10 The use of transmission controls in message framing.

national Telex Network where it is frequently known as the telex code or as CCITT (Comité Consultatif International Télégraphique et Téléphonique) Alphabet no. 2.

The Baudot code is a five bit code, which means that it can represent 32 characters. This is not enough for a full alphanumeric character set and the character handling capability of the code has to be expanded. This is done by designating two of the characters as code extension characters. The code extension characters are known as the letter shift character (LS) and the figure shift character (FS). The letter shift is binary 11111 (Fig. 1.12) and the figure shift is binary 11011 (Fig. 1.12). These code extension characters tell the receiver which column of Fig. 1.12 to use when interpreting an incoming stream of data.

If a figure shift (FS) appears in a character stream, the characters following it are interpreted as though they have the meaning in the figures character column of Fig. 1.12. If a letter shift occurs in a character stream, the characters following the letter shift are interpreted as though they have the meaning in the letter character column of Fig. 1.12. The figure shift (FS) and letter shift (LS) characters operate in a similar manner to the 'shift lock' and 'shift release' keys on a typewriter, where pressing the 'shift lock' keys causes all the letters following to be typed in upper case until the 'shift release' key is pressed. Devices using the Baudot code must include some sort of 'memory' in order to 'remember' whether the figure shift or letter shift mode is in operation.

The Baudot code is slightly cumbersome and would probably not be chosen today for computer and digital communications. It was originally developed for natural language (mainly text) and at the time when mechanical limitations restricted bit rates to less than 30 bits per second. However, the

TC₁   *SOH Start of heading*—a transmission control character used as the first character of a heading of an information message.

TC₂   *STX Start of text*—a transmission control character which precedes a text and which is used to terminate a heading.

TC₃   *ETX End of text*—a transmission control character which terminates a text.

TC₄   *EOT End of transmission*—a transmission control character used to indicate the conclusion of the transmission of one or more texts.

TC₅   *ENQ ENQUIRY*—a transmission control character used as a request for a response from a remote station—the response may include station identification and/or station status.

TC₆   *ACK Acknowledge*—a transmission control character transmitted by a receiver as an affirmative response to the sender.

TC₇   *DLE Data link escape*—a transmission control character which will change the meaning of a limited number of contiguously following characters. It is used exclusively to provide supplementary data transmission control functions. Only graphics and transmission control characters can be used in DLE sequences.

TC₈   *NAK Negative acknowledge*—a transmission control character transmitted by a receiver as a negative response to the sender.

TC₉   *SYN Synchronous idle*—a transmission control character used by a synchronous transmission system in the absence of any other character (idle condition) to provide a signal from which synchronism may be achieved or retained between terminal equipments.

TC₁₀   *ETB End of transmission block*—a transmission control character used to indicate the end of a transmission block of data where data is divided into such blocks for transmission purposes.

Fig. 1.11 The transmission control characters.

Baudot code is still important and is used in many international telex systems.

1.7 ERROR DETECTION SCHEMES

There are three main error detection schemes. These are (1) parity bit, (2) two co-ordinate parity check and (3) cyclic redundancy checks.

1.7.1 Parity bit

Although the characters in the ASCII format only require seven bits (bit 1 to 7), eight bits are sometimes transmitted. The eighth bit is known as the parity

Binary	Letters Characters	Figures Characters
00000	Blank	Blank
00001	E	3
00010	≡	≡ Line feed
00011	A	−
00100	SP	SP Space
00101	S	′
00110	I	8
00111	U	7
01000	<	< Carriage return
01001	D	⊹ Who are you?
01010	R	4
01011	J	℞ Bell
01100	N	,
01101	F	%
01110	C	:
01111	K	(
10000	T	5
10001	Z	+
10010	L	)
10011	″	2
10100	H	£
10101	Y	6
10110	P	0
10111	Q	1
11000	O	9
11001	B	?
11010	G	$
11011	↑	↑ Figure shift (FS)
11100	M	.
11101	X	/
11110	V	=
11111	↓	↓ Letter shift (LS)

Fig. 1.12 Baudot code.

bit and its purpose is to provide some error detection capability. Parity can be *even* or *odd*. A character has even parity if all the 1s in the character (including the parity bit) add up to an even number. A character has odd parity if all the 1s in it (including the parity bit) add up to an odd number.

The way the parity system works is quite simple. The transmitting terminal appends a parity bit to each character and transmits the encoded character along the communications line starting with the least significant bit (bit 1). As the receiver receives the seven data bits, it computes its own parity bit. The receiver then compares its computed parity bit with the received parity bit and, if they match, it declares the character valid.

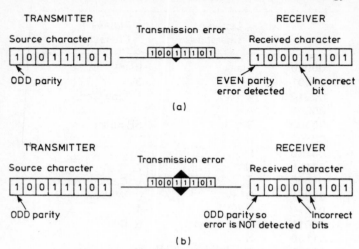

Fig. 1.13 ASCII character parity checking.
(a) Single bit reversed.
(b) Two bits reversed.

Figure 1.13(a) illustrates the sequence of events that occurs if a transmission error takes place while a character is being sent. Based on the first seven bits it receives the receiver computes a parity bit of 0 but receives a parity bit of 1. The receiver therefore knows that a transmission error has occurred.

If two bits are in error, as shown in Fig. 1.13(b), the receiver will not detect the error because the incoming character will pass the character parity check. From this, you should note that the simple character parity procedure is not foolproof, because it can only detect changes in odd numbers of bits.

If changes occur in an even number of bits the parity check will be passed and the receiver will assume that it has received a valid character. More sophisticated methods have to be used to detect multiple errors. Note also that parity checking does not provide a means for correcting the error.

1.7.2   Two co-ordinate parity check

The inability of the simple character parity check to detect even numbers of bit errors within a character has led to a slightly more sophisticated method of parity checking called the *two co-ordinate parity check*. Figure 1.14 shows a block of data containing fourteen characters. The characters are being transmitted with each character having its own parity bit (column P). In this system, the character parity check is known as the *horizontal* parity bit, the *transverse* parity bit, the *lateral* parity bit or the *row* parity bit. Note that the parity is *odd* for the example of Fig. 1.14.

When these fourteen characters have been transmitted, a block check character (BCC) is sent. This block contains eight bits. Bits 1 to 7 constitute the

Bit ⟶

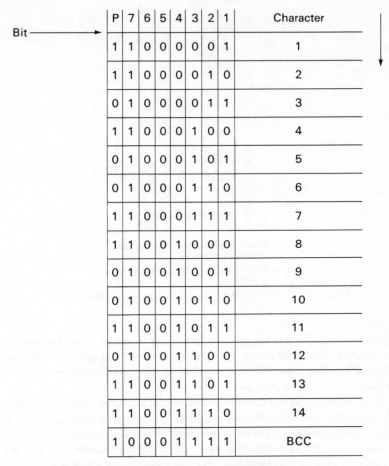

P	7	6	5	4	3	2	1	Character
1	1	0	0	0	0	0	1	1
1	1	0	0	0	0	1	0	2
0	1	0	0	0	0	1	1	3
1	1	0	0	0	1	0	0	4
0	1	0	0	0	1	0	1	5
0	1	0	0	0	1	1	0	6
1	1	0	0	0	1	1	1	7
1	1	0	0	1	0	0	0	8
0	1	0	0	1	0	0	1	9
0	1	0	0	1	0	1	0	10
1	1	0	0	1	0	1	1	11
0	1	0	0	1	1	0	0	12
1	1	0	0	1	1	0	1	13
1	1	0	0	1	1	1	0	14
1	0	0	0	1	1	1	1	BCC

Fig. 1.14 Two co-ordinate parity check.

parity bits respectively for columns 1 to 7 of the preceding fourteen characters. For example, BCC bit 1 is the parity bit for all the bit 1s of the preceding fourteen characters. BCC bit 2 is the parity bit for all the bit 2s of the preceding fourteen characters. BCC bit 3 is the parity bit for all the bit 3s of the preceding fourteen characters, etc. These parity bits are often called, the *longitudinal* parity bit, the *column* parity bit or the *vertical* parity bit. Note that in this case, *even* parity has been chosen for *column* parity bits 1 to 7.

BCC bit 8 is not the column parity bit for all the parity bits of the preceding characters. BCC bit 8 is actually the row parity bit for the seven bits of the BCC character. This *row* parity bit is *odd* because all the previous row parity bits were odd.

You are now in a position to examine Fig. 1.15 to see how the *block check character* helps to detect additional errors. In this figure, the single bit error in character 2 would be detected by both the horizontal and the vertical

Bit	P	7	6	5	4	3	2	1	Character
	1	0	1	0	1	1	0	1	1
	1	0	0	[0]	. 1	0	0	0	2
	0	1	0	0	0	1	0	1	3
	0	0	1	1	1	0	0	0	4
	0	1	0	1	1	0	1	1	5
	1	1	1	1	0	(0	0)	1	6
	0	1	1	0	1	(1	1)	0	7
	1	0	0	1	0	1	1	1	8
	0	[0	0]	0	1	0	1	1	9
	0	0	1	0	0	1	1	0	10
	1	1	0	1	0	1	1	0	BCC

P = Parity bit

$\begin{pmatrix} 0 & 0 \\ 1 & 1 \end{pmatrix}$ = Error bit(s) undetected

$\boxed{0}$ = Error detected by longitudinal and lateral parity

$\boxed{0 \ 0}$ = Error detected by longitudinal parity only

Fig. 1.15 Error detection by two co-ordinate parity.

parity check. The double bit error in character 9 would be picked up by the vertical parity check. However, the four bit error in characters 6 and 7 would get through undetected. Thus the system is still not foolproof but it does allow more errors to be detected.

Two co-ordinate parity checking is frequently used because it is relatively cheap to implement with electronic circuitry. The main disadvantage of the two co-ordinate system is that it involves an increased amount of overhead in the form of one bit for each character plus an extra character at the end of each block of characters. However, the situation can be analysed mathematically and, for a given line with a given error rate, an optimum block length can be computed to give maximum throughput for a desired undetected error rate.

1.7.3   Cyclic redundancy check

The *cyclic redundancy check* treats all data transmitted as one long binary number, regardless of whether it is a string of characters or whether it is a pure binary bit stream. This long binary number is then divided by another binary number called the *constant* in a modulo two division (see Fig. 1.16). This process of dividing the data by the constant yields a *quotient* and a *remainder*. The quotient is discarded but the remainder is transmitted down the line immediately after the data. At the receiving end, the received data is initially treated as a pure binary number and modulo divided by the same constant to yield a quotient and a remainder. The quotient is discarded but the computed remainder is compared against the received remainder. If the

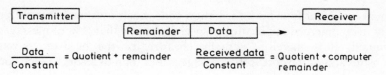

Fig. 1.16 Cyclic redundancy check.

two match, the data is declared valid; if the two do not match, the data is declared erroneous. You should note that a match is no guarantee that there is no error because there could have been two or more errors in the transmission which compensated for each other. However, this is a relatively rare event.

1.8   ERROR CORRECTION

When an error has been detected, it is desirable to take some form of action that will either correct the error or at least minimise its effect. The three main error correction methods are (1) symbol substitution, (2) forward error correction and (3) retransmission.

1.8.1   Symbol substitution

For the many cases when the data is intended to be read by a human operator, a simple character parity check is used. If an error is detected, the erroneous character is simply replaced by the SUB character in the ASCII table of Fig. 1.9 which is often printed as a reverse question mark or a sequence of three vertical lines. The human operator then corrects the error. For example, a statement received as:

IT IS N?CE TO HAVE SUNS?INE.

can be easily interpreted as:

IT IS NICE TO HAVE SUNSHINE.

This method of correction can be used for word processing applications of computer networks when the final destination is a human being.

1.8.2   Forward error correction

Forward error correction codes involve the use of special transmission codes that contain sufficient redundant information so that any detected errors can be corrected at the receiving end. There are a number of codes which permit this type of operation. For example, one of the best-known error correcting codes is the Hamming code (after R. W. Hamming) which uses three additional bits for a four bit information code. Such overheads are extremely costly in commercial applications especially· as less than 1% of messages are corrupted. It is therefore actually cheaper for the receiver to request retransmission of the corrupted message rather than to resort to such codes.

1.8.3   Retransmission

Retransmission is by far the commonest means of error correction. Simply speaking, when the receiver detects a block of erroneous data it asks the sender to retransmit and hopefully this second transmission will be received without error. If the second transmission is still received in error, then further transmissions may be requested.

1.9   TRANSMISSION MODES

There are two main transmission modes: (1) parallel transmission and (2) serial transmission. Serial transmission can be subdivided into asynchronous and synchronous transmission.

1.9.1   Parallel transmission

Most computers work in the parallel mode (Fig. 1.17) in the sense that all the bits needed to represent a character are transmitted simultaneously. This method allows efficient and fast transmission of signals. Parallel transmission is often used for on-site communications and for the transmission of data between the computer and its nearby peripherals, such as disk handlers and keyboards. Over long distances, parallel transmission presents problems because the cost of these parallel channels becomes expensive.

If you wish, you may compare parallel transmission to a motorway where there are many traffic lanes and all vehicles travel along very quickly at the same speed. However, the many additional traffic lanes cost money and motorways are expensive to build. Serial transmission is more like the case where there is only one traffic lane. Vehicles move along more slowly and

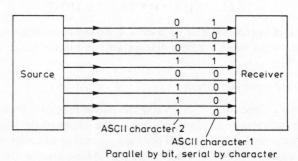

Fig. 1.17 Parallel transmission.

their speed of movement must be more carefully controlled but single lanes are less expensive to build.

1.9.2　Serial transmission

In serial transmission (Fig. 1.18), character bits are transmitted one after another along one channel. The receiver then reassembles the incoming bit stream into characters. Serial transmission presents two synchronisation problems to the receiver: bit synchronisation and character synchronisation.

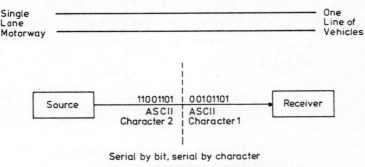

Fig. 1.18　Serial transmission.

(a)　Bit synchronisation

Consider the serial transmission data being sent in Fig. 1.19(a). To interpret this data correctly, the receiver must (1) measure or sample the data in synchronism with the data rate (bits per second) at which the data is being sent and (2) sample the data at approximately a steady state value point (Fig. 1.18(b)) on the waveform, e.g., the centre point of each bit. Point (1) is important because if sampling is carried out too slowly then some of the bits will be missed; alternatively too fast sampling will cause more bits to be sampled than were sent. Point (2) is important because if sampling was taken at the 0 to 1 or 1 to 0 transition points then the indeterminate values resulting could cause errors. Waveforms also deteriorate when sent over long distances and sampling is best carried out at the mid-points of each bit where waveform distortion is minimal.

(b)　Character synchronisation

In Fig. 1.18 two eight bit characters are being transmitted serially along the communications line. In this figure, the two groups of eight bits belonging to the characters have been labelled separately. However the bit stream is not labelled in this manner when it appears at the receiving device. The receiver

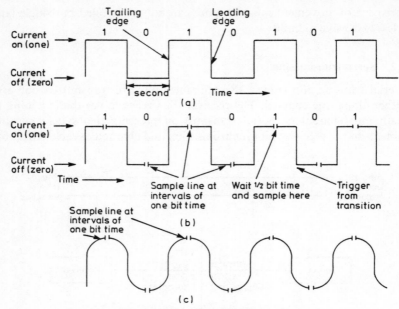

Fig. 1.19 Bit synchronisation and sampling.
(a) Serial data transmission.
(b) Sampling.
(c) Wave form after transmission deterioration.

must determine (1) the starting bit of each character, (2) the number of bits in each character and (3) the rate at which the bits are sent.

Items (2) and (3) can be solved by an agreement (protocol) between the sender and the receiver prior to the transmission of signals. The receiver then merely has to identify the first bit of each character, count off the required number of bits per character at the correct transmission rate and re-assemble the characters. Item (1), the starting bit of each character, is identified by synchronisation and will be explained in detail in section 1.10.3 on synchronisation procedures.

1.10   TRANSMISSION SYNCHRONISATION

There are two common approaches to determining which bit is the first bit of an incoming character. One approach uses a technique known as asynchronous transmission and the other technique is known as synchronous transmission.

1.10.1   Asynchronous transmission

Asynchronous (start/stop) transmission is used in systems in which char-

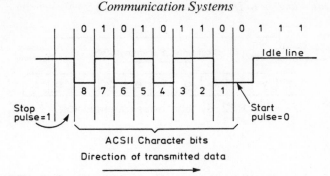

Fig. 1.20 One character transmitted asynchronously.

acters are sent one at a time without necessarily having any fixed time relationship between one character and the next. A typical example of such a case is that of a person typing. Each press of a key produces a character but the speed (data rate) at which the keys are pressed varies according to the speed of the typist. In such a case (Fig. 1.20), the source sends a start bit followed by the character bits and then at least one stop bit. This is to inform the receiver that a character is to follow after the start bit whilst the stop bit after the character is to inform the receiver that the bits for that character has ended. The next character sent is also preceded by a start bit and ended by a stop bit. This enables the receiver to identify each character as it is received. Such a mode of transmission is shown in Fig. 1.21.

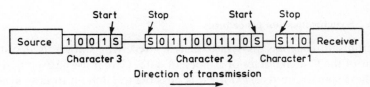

Fig. 1.21 Asynchronous transmission.

1.10.2 Synchronous transmission

Synchronous transmission is used to transmit complete blocks of data at one time. In synchronous transmission, the duration of each bit is the same and, in character transmission systems, the time interval between the end of the last bit of a character and the beginning of the first bit of the next character is either zero time or a whole multiple of the time required to transmit a complete character. Figure 1.22 shows how the letters of the alphabet can be transmitted using synchronous transmission. With all of the characters joined together with zero time between them the receiver needs only to identify the first bit of the first character and then, knowing the *character size* and

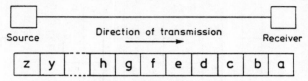

Fig. 1.22 Synchronous transmission.

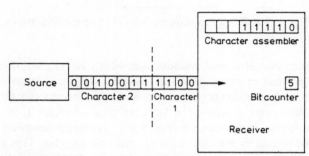

Fig. 1.23 Synchronous transmission–receiver counts off bits for each character.

transmission rate, count off groups of bits correctly and reassemble the incoming bits into characters. This is shown in Fig. 1.23.

1.10.3   Synchronisation procedures

Synchronisation signals are sent to enable a receiving station to identify the first bit of the first character of a block of data. Care must be exercised as to how these signals are received for it is possible to latch on to false synchronisation signals if the correct procedure is not followed.

(a) True synchronisation

The key to this problem is of course identifying the first bit of the first character. To identify correctly the first bit of the first character, each block of data is preceded with a unique synchronising pattern. This makes use of the SYN transmission control character (TC$_9$ in Fig. 1.9). The SYN character has a bit pattern of 00010110 (with odd parity) and the receiver is designed to sample continually the latest set of eight bits that it has received and to compare these bits with the unique SYN pattern. If this SYN pattern is detected two or more times consecutively, then the receiver declares itself synchronised and it is ready to receive synchronous messages. This is shown in Fig. 1.24. In practice, the source usually sends three or four SYN characters to ensure that the receiver will detect at least two.

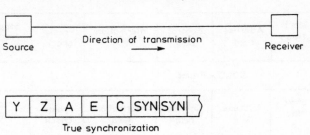

Fig. 1.24 Two SYNs guard against false synchronisation.

(b) False synchronisation

If the receiver is unable to detect a consecutive SYN signal immediately after the first SYN signal then false synchronisation results. The receiver declares false synchronisation and carries on in the 'Look for sync' mode until it achieves synchronisation.

False synchronisation can be understood if reference is made to Fig. 1.25. In this figure, a stream of characters, c, b, a, z, y, x, are being sent from the source to the receiver. The receiver constantly compares the latest eight bits it has received against the SYN signal pattern and it can find such a pattern by

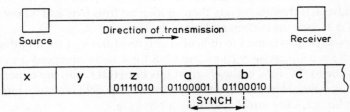

Fig. 1.25 False synchronisation.

using the last four bits of the letter 'b' and the first four bits of the letter 'a'. However, the next eight bits (last four bits of 'a' and first four bits of 'z') do not constitute the consecutive SYN pattern of bits required, hence it knows that false synchronisation has been achieved.

1.11 BINARY SYNCHRONOUS COMMUNICATIONS LINKS

In binary synchronous communications links, synchronisation is established before the message is sent and is checked and adjusted during transmission.

Typical examples of synchronous communications links are SDLC (synchronous data link control) and HDLC (high-level data link control). SDLC was developed by a commercial organisation (IBM) for the exchange of data

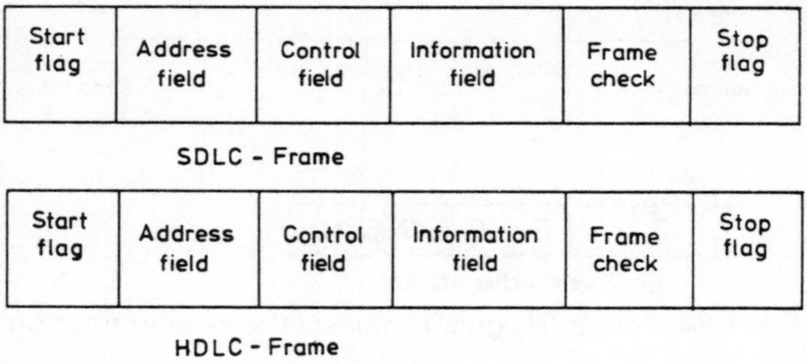

Start flag	Address field	Control field	Information field	Frame check	Stop flag

SDLC - Frame

Start flag	Address field	Control field	Information field	Frame check	Stop flag

HDLC - Frame

Fig. 1.26

in their communications link. HDLC is a communications system recognised by the International Systems Organisation (ISO) for synchronous communications and is used in many transmission systems. It is similar to SDLC and is used for full duplex transmissions.

In SDLC and HDLC, messages are formatted into frames of information as shown in Fig. 1.26. Each frame is divided into fields. The first field in any frame is a flag or code consisting of a binary sequence 01111110. The next field is the address field which identifies the sending or receiving station. The SDLC address is always eight bits long, but the HDLC address can be any length. The receiver can determine the length by examining the first bit in each address. If the first bit is 0, then another address byte will follow it. If the first bit is 1, then the current address is the last.

The control field is used to indicate the type of frame; I for an information frame, S for a supervisory frame, and NS for a non-sequenced transmission frame. The SDLC field is always eight bits but HDLC can use either eight or sixteen bit fields. Here again, if the first bit is 0, the field is sixteen bits long. If the first bit is 1, the control field is eight bits long.

The information field can consist of a bit stream of any length. No breaks in the information field are allowed. If the transmitting equipment does not receive a continuing stream of bits from the data equipment, it will abort the message. The abort signal is 11111111 for SDLC and 01111111 for HDLC.

It is legitimate to endorse characters such as 01111110 within the information field but to prevent these characters from being mistaken as control characters, the transmitter automatically inserts a 0 following five consecutive 1s in the data stream. For example 01111110 would be transmitted as 011111010. (This technique is sometimes called 'bit stuffing'.) The receiver automatically removes the added 0 after a consecutive string of five 1s. Hence 011111010 would be recognised as 01111110 which is the ~ symbol in ASCII code.

The frame check character is a means of error detection. The character is calculated using the bit pattern of the address, control and information fields. The frame is terminated by a stop flag, binary 01111110. An idle pattern; a continuous high level on the data line is transmitted between frames.

1.12 BUFFERED TERMINALS

Another problem frequently encountered with synchronous transmission is that data is often transmitted at a faster rate than that which the receiver can utilise directly. For example, some printers are unable to cope directly with a data rate of 9600 bits per second (bps). In such cases, the data sent to the printer is stored in buffers until it can be used.

There is also a limit to the amount of storage which a buffer can hold and, in such cases, flow control characters are used to inform the sender when to stop and restart transmission. Such procedures are known as protocols and will be discussed more extensively later in the book.

1.13 TRANSMISSION EFFICIENCY

Synchronous transmission makes very good use of the data carrying capacity of a communications line because most of the data it sends after initial synchronising is usable data. Asynchronous data is less efficient because it carries extensive 'overheads'. For example, in the case of an ASCII transmission, with eight bits being transmitted for every character plus an overhead of one start bit and one stop bit, a total of ten bits is required for every character. However, only eight of the ten bits constitute useful data, therefore the maximum possible efficiency is

$$8/10 \times 100 = 80\%$$

To reinforce this point further, I will compare the transmission efficiency of a synchronous and an asynchronous system for sending a block of 480 ASCII characters. For the synchronous system, I shall assume that each block of data is preceded by three SYN characters. The bit content of each block is:

3 SYN characters × 8 bits per character = 24 bits
Total number of bits transmitted = 3864 bits

The ratio of information bits transferred to the total number of bits transmitted is:

$$3840/3864 \times 100 = 99.4\%$$

The efficiency for asynchronous transmission has already been calculated at 80%, therefore synchronous transmission is $99.4 - 80 = 19.4\%$, more efficient than asynchronous transmission in this case.

In conclusion, synchronous transmission is used whenever possible because of its more efficient use of the communications channel. Asynchronous transmission is used in cases where interrupted data (e.g. typing data) is generated, and/or to maintain compatibility with the immense number of asynchronous terminals still in use.

CHAPTER 2
Interfaces and Protocols

2.0 INTERFACES AND PROTOCOLS

This chapter deals with the more commonly encountered interfaces; these include several European, American and Japanese standards.

2.1 INTRODUCTION

Your brain is a marvellous instrument because it is capable of carrying out many functions automatically. In the case of a conversation between you and another person, your brain does the following automatically:

(1) *Modulation* – converts your thoughts into electrical signals within your brain, followed by actuation of your voice box to produce speech for transmission through the air medium. The changing of signals from one type to another is called modulation.
(2) *Signal compatibility* – selects a language understood by your listener.
(3) *Signal strength* – selects a speech level which can be heard by your listener.
(4) *Data rate* – selects a speech rate which can be understood by your listener.
(5) *Protocol* – decides when to speak and when to listen, i.e. controls the flow rate of information.
(6) *Demodulation* – receives speech signals and reconverts them to signals understood by the brain.

These processes, initially introduced in Chapter 1, are general to most communication systems, and computers wishing to communicate with each other or with their peripherals also follow similar procedures.

In order to facilitate discussion between the various types of computer communications, several terms must be defined. Consider the case in Fig. 2.1, where computer A is to communicate with computer B via ordinary telephone lines. It can be shown by mathematical analysis (Fourier series) that the digital signals from a computer operating at 1200 bits per second can contain a direct current, a fundamental frequency of half the digital rate (600 Hz) and an infinite number of harmonics of this fundamental frequency. The frequency difference between the highest signal frequency and the lowest signal frequency, called frequency bandwidth, is too large for direct transmission through the nominal 3 kHz bandwidth of a telephone line. The computer signals must therefore be modified by modem A into a signal form suitable for transmission through the telephone lines.

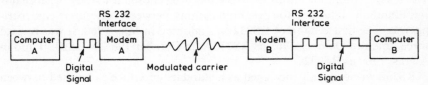

Fig. 2.1 Data link with modems.

The signals received via the telephone lines at modem B are not directly suitable for computer B and they must be demodulated into a digital form suitable for computer B. In order to specify the work to be carried out by each, demarcation lines are drawn between pieces of equipment. Such demarcation lines are known as interfaces.

2.2 INTERFACES

An interface can be defined as the line of demarcation between two pieces of equipment. For two pieces of equipment to work harmoniously, they must each obey a complementary set of interface specifications. Interface specifications include many things, from the physical specifications of the connectors to electrical signals and to the procedures or protocols which the signals must use to exchange information. A detailed study of the many standard interfaces available is beyond the scope of this book. A list of the better known interfaces described by the Comité Consultatif International Télégraphique et Téléphonique (CCITT), an international organisation which specifies recommendations for these interfaces, is given in appendices C and D. Appendix C lists some of the 'V' set of recommendations which deal mainly with present day analogue communications systems. Appendix D lists some of the 'X' set of recommendations which deal mainly with digital communications.

CCITT recommendations are 'de facto' standards used by the national bodies and manufacturers of many countries. They are not called standards for political reasons. Standards would be binding on the countries concerned whereas recommendations may be ignored when convenient.

A rudimentary knowledge of most interfaces can be obtained by considering their four most important characteristics. These are:

(1) Mechanical – connectors, cabling, etc.
(2) Electrical – signal type, amplitude, etc.

(3) Functional – purpose of signals.
(4) Procedural – control and timing.

2.3 RS232 COMMUNICATIONS INTERFACE

The RS232 communications interface has been chosen for study because it is the dominant interface for communications between computers and peripherals. The first version of RS232 was adopted in May 1960. It was revised three times: in October 1963 as RS232A, in October 1965 as RS232B and in August 1969 as RS232C.

RS232 was originally designed as a standard interface to be used between data terminal equipment and modems (see Fig. 2.1). However, it has been freely adapted to be used for other purposes, e.g., communications between a computer and a printer. The important characteristics of RS232 will be discussed in the following sections.

2.3.1 Mechanical

The mechanical aspects pertain to the point of demarcation, which is usually the pluggable connector. The one usually used for this interface is the 25 pin connector shown in Fig. 2.2. However, be warned, some manufacturers claim

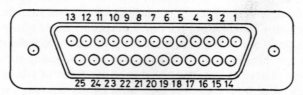

Fig. 2.2

RS232 compatibility but do not use this connector. The full RS232C specifications define twenty-one interchange circuits, but some manufacturers do not provide the full twenty-one circuits. Each associated circuit is assigned a pin connection on the standard 25 pin plug. These are shown in Fig. 2.3 but this figure requires some explanation. The first column refers to the subsection of the CCITT specifications where a full explanation of the circuits designated in column 2 may be obtained. The letters within brackets in the first column refer to the EIA (Electronics Industries Association) designations and specifications for the circuits of column 2. Column 2 lists the name of the circuits; column 3 lists the pin numbers and column 4 lists the abbreviations commonly used with these circuits.

RS232 also specifies that cable lengths between connecting devices must be

V.24 (RS232) Circuit	Name	Pin Number	Abbreviations
101 (AA)	Cable Screen	1	GND
102 (AB)	Signal ground or common return	7	SIG GND
103 (BA)	Transmitted data	2	XMT
104 (BB)	Received data	3	RCV
105 (CA)	Request to send	4	RTS
106 (CB)	Ready for sending (Clear to send)	5	CTS
107 (CC)	Data set ready	6	DSR
108 (CD)	Connect data set to line/Data terminal ready	20	DTR
109 (CF)	Data channel received line signal detector	8	DCD
110 (CG)	Data signal quality detector	–	
111 (CH)	Data signalling rate selector (DTE source)	23	DRS
113 (DA)	Transmitter signal element timing (DTE source)	24	
114 (DB)	Transmitter signal element timing (DCE source)	15	X CLK
115 (DD)	Receiver signal element timing (DCE source)	17	R CLK
116	Select standby	(24)	
118 (SBA)	Transmitted backward channel data	14	XMT
119 (SBB)	Received backward channel data	16	RCV
120 (SCA)	Transmit backward channel line signal	19	RTS
121 (SCB)	Backward channel ready	13	CTS
122 (SCF)	Backward channel received line signal detector	12	DCD
125 (CE)	Calling indicator	22	RI
126	Select transmit frequency	11	STF
140	Remote loopback for point-to-point circuits	21	
141	Local loopback	18	
142	Test indicator	25	BY

Fig. 2.3 Pin assignments in 25-way connector for RS232.

limited to a maximum of 15 m. This length is specified because signal loss (attenuation) and waveform distortion increase with length.

2.3.2 Electrical

Data is transmitted in serial format in the RS232 interface. The data transmitted can be synchronous or asynchronous. RS232 does not specify the data transmission code which must be used and codes using five to eight bits plus a parity bit are frequently used in transmission. One of the more popular codes used for this interface is ASCII, and I have chosen this code in Fig. 2.4 to

Fig. 2.4 Serial data transmission of ASCII data.

explain how one type of data may be transmitted in an asynchronous mode in this interface. Details will vary with other transmission codes but the general principles remain similar.

In Fig. 2.4, a logic 1 signal is known as the *mark* condition and is the *idle* state. The beginning of data transmission is signalled by a transition to the logic 0 or *space* condition. One space serves as the prefix or *start* bit of the data transmission. Seven bits of ASCII data are then transmitted in succession, starting with the least significant bit and ending with the most significant bit. This is immediately followed by a parity bit. Stop bits of logic 1 denote the end of transmission. Normally two stop bits are used followed immediately by a start bit if a new character is ready to be sent or followed by a mark condition if no character is ready.

2.3.3   Data and signalling rates

Before discussing the signalling rates used in the RS232 interface, I would like to explain the difference between the data transmission rate and the signalling rate of a digital transmission system.

The rate at which a serial digital transmission system exchanges data is measured in binary digits or bits per second. This is called the data transmission rate or data rate. For example, if the data transmission rate of a system is 2400 bits per second, it means that 2400 bits are transmitted every second. The rate at which a serial digital system changes signalling rates is expressed as states per second or baud. For example, if there are 2400 signalling states per second, the signalling rate of the system is 2400 baud.

If one change in signalling rate represents one data bit change, then the signalling rate and the data transmission rate are the same. This is true for a binary signalling system, where a change in signalling rate represents one digit. In this particular case, it can be said that a signalling rate of 2400 baud represents a data rate of 2400.

If one change in signalling rate represents two digital bit changes, then the data transmission rate is twice that of the signalling rate. For this case, if the signalling rate is 2400, then the data rate is 4800.

The above is important because the maximum signalling rate in a transmission system is limited by its bandwidth. However, certain modulation techniques (e.g. quadrature modulation phase modulation, described in Chapter 6) do allow the data transmission rate to be greater than the signalling rate.

The specifications in the RS232 document refer to signalling rates or baud. The common baud rates used in the interface are 75, 110, 150, 300, 600, 1200, 2400, 4800, 9600. You can use the baud rate to calculate the character rate of transmission. For example, assume that transmission is taking place at 110 baud and that each character is made up of the bits shown in Fig. 2.4, i.e. eleven bits: one start bit, seven data bits, one parity bit and two stop bits. The character transmission rate is therefore $110/11 = 10$ characters per second.

This information can be used to select a printer which can keep up with the rate of data transfer.

2.3.4 Logic signal levels

Negative true logic signals are used in the RS232 standard; the amplitude levels are shown in Fig. 2.5. A logic 1 level is in the range of -5 to $-15\,\text{V}$. A logic 0 is in the range of $+5$ to $+15\,\text{V}$.

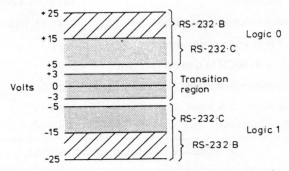

Fig. 2.5 RS232 voltage levels, inverted so that a negative level represents a logic 1 and a positive level a logic 0. Signals in the transition region between $+3$ and -3 are not defined.

Transmitted signals are often attenuated when they arrive at the receiver. Hence RS232 receivers must recognise signals as low as $+3\,\text{V}$ as logic 0 and as high as $-3\,\text{V}$ as logic 1. Further RS232 specifications are given in Fig. 2.6. Most of the terms used therein are self-explanatory, but I wish to point out particularly that the maximum load capacitance may not exceed 2500 pF. This is important because multiconductor cable exhibits a capacitance of about 150 pF per metre which means that RS232 transmission cannot be used (strictly speaking) for distances exceeding 2500/150 or 17 m. Most manufacturers quote 15 m as the maximum cable length for this interface.

2.3.5 Functional

A comprehensive list of functions for this interface has already been introduced in Fig. 2.3. A full description of each and every function is not possible here but the often used functions shown in Fig. 2.7 will be discussed. These functions may be classified as follows.

(1) Functions sent from the data terminal equipment (DTE), the generic name for terminals or computers, to the data circuit terminating equipment (DCE), the generic name for the modem and its accessories. These are:

Driver output levels with 3 to 7-kΩ load	logic 0: + 5 to + 15 V logic 1: − 5 to − 15 V
Driver output voltage with no load	− 25 to + 25 V
Driver output impedance with power off	greater than 300 Ω
Output short circuit current	less than 0.5 A
Driver slew rate	less than 30 V/μs
Receiver input impedance	between 3 and 7 kΩ
Allowable receiver input voltage range	− 25 to + 25 V
Receiver output with open circuit input	logic 1
Receiver output with 300Ω to ground on input	logic 1
Receiver output with + 3-V input	logic 0
Receiver output with − 3-V input	logic 1
Maximum load capacitance	2500 pF

Fig. 2.6 RS232C electrical specifications.

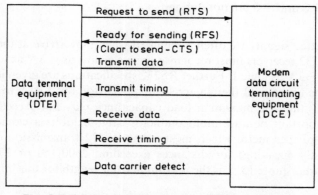

Fig. 2.7 Main components of RS232 interface.

    (i) *Request to send* (*RTS*) – the data terminal equipment (DTE) sends this signal to the modem when it wants to transmit data.

   (ii) *Transmitted data* – this wire from the DTE to the modem carries the digital data that is to be modulated onto the carrier.

(2) Functions sent from the data circuit terminating equipment (DCE) to the data terminal equipment (DTE) include:

    (i) *Clear to send* (*CTS*) – this signal from the modem informs the data terminal equipment that it can start to transmit.

   (ii) *Transmit timing* – this signal from the modem to the data equipment provides timing signals to the terminal so that data is clocked out of the terminal at the correct speed.

(iii) *Receive data* – this wire carries the digital data from the modem to the data terminal equipment. This is the data the modem has demodulated from the carrier.

(iv) *Receive timing* – this signal from the modem to the data terminal equipment accompanies the data so that the terminal equipment knows when to sample the incoming received data stream to interpret correctly the bits. The receive timing is derived from the carrier by the modem.

(v) *Data carrier detect* – this signal from the modem to the DTE advises the DTE that the modem has locked on to the received carrier and that it is ready to demodulate data.

2.3.6 Procedural

The procedural section deals with the control of data signals and the timing of signals within the RS232C interface. I shall illustrate this with the example shown in Fig. 2.8. In this example, data from DTE 'A' is to be sent to DTE 'B'. The protocol, the set of rules that governs the flow of data, is as follows:

(1) DTE 'A' sends the 'request to send (RTS)' signal to modem 'A'. Modem 'A' gets ready for transmission by sending the carrier wave (a sinewave signal that will carry the computer signals) along the connecting line. After a time delay Tp, the carrier wave arrives at the input of modem 'B'. Modem 'B' realises that there is a carrier on the line, locks onto the carrier and synchronises itself to the signal. Demodulation of data by modem 'B' is now possible. Modem 'B' signals this to DTE 'B' by raising the data carrier detect (DCD) signal. The DCD 'on delay' in Fig. 2.8 is effectively the time it takes modem 'B' to recognise the presence of the incoming carrier.

(2) In order to give the receiving modem (modem 'B') time to lock onto the carrier, the transmitting modem (modem 'A') delays sending a 'clear to send (CTS)' signal back to its own transmitting DTE 'A'. The amount of time delay is determined either by a timing device within modem 'A' or by the reception of a signal from modem 'B'. In either case, this delay is set to be longer than the DCD 'on delay'. The CTS signal informs DTE 'A' that it can proceed to send data. DTE 'A' sends its data, which is modulated onto the carrier wave by modem 'A'. The modulated carrier travels along the line and is demodulated by the receiving modem (modem 'B') which passes the data onto the receiving DTE 'B'.

(3) DTE 'B' requires some reaction time to realise that it has received data and must begin to act on the data received. This delay is known as the terminal equipment 'reaction time'. The total time from the end of the reaction time to the time when the receiving DTE initiates the transmission of the response message is called the 'processing time'.

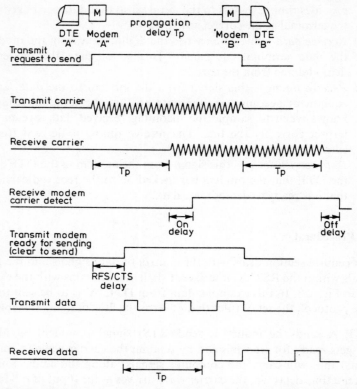

Fig. 2.8 Modem timing – two-wire operation showing the effect of propagation delay (T_p).

(4) When the sending terminal (DTE 'A') has finished transmitting its data, it removes the 'request to send' signal to modem 'A'. Modem 'A' drops its carrier wave and the 'clear to send' signal to DTE 'A'.

(5) At the receiving end modem 'B', sensing the disappearance of both carrier and data, will (after a short delay) remove its 'data carrier detect' signal to DTE 'B'. This delay, known as 'DCD off' delay, is incorporated to allow the receiving modem to coast through a momentary carrier dropout without notifying the receiving DTE 'B' that there has been a loss of carrier.

(6) The whole process is then repeated in the opposite direction in order to get the response back to the sending terminal (DTE 'A'). The roles of transmitter and receiver are reversed. DTE 'B' now sends 'request to send' to modem 'B'. Modem 'B' sends the carrier along to the input of modem 'A', as well as a 'clear to send' signal (after a short delay) to DTE 'B'. At the new receiving end, modem A sends the DCD signal, followed (after a short delay) by the demodulated signal to DTE 'A'. At the end of data transmission DTE 'B' removes its 'request to send' signal, which in

turn drops the carrier signal and the 'clear to send' signal from modem 'B'.

(a) Timing

The data rate of signals, the propagation time of signals along the line and the time delays associated with the different modems vary from device to device. These are set up by the operator for the particular type of equipment used. I can only give you representative times.

(1) *Data rate* – the data rate used is one of the standard RS232C rates. The sending and the receiving ends must both use the same data rate for a given direction of transmission.
(2) *Propagation delay time* – this is the time it takes to get the signal from one end of the line to the other. On terrestrial lines, this delay is about 6 to 9 $\mu s\,km^{-1}$.
(3) *Modem delay time* – this is the time when the digital signal is presented to the RS232 interface until the modulated carrier appears on the line. There is also a similar delay when the receiving modem demodulates the incoming signal. The delay varies according to the type of modem used but a figure of 10 to 15 ms per modem pair is normal.
(4) *Reaction time* – this is the time it takes for each DTE to realise that it has received data and that an acknowledgement has to be sent.

(b) Half and full duplex transmission

The system described above is that for the case when the RS232 interface is used for half duplex working. Full duplex working at 1200 baud rate through two wire telephone lines is not generally possible because of the limited bandwidth of two wire telephone transmission lines.

(c) Asymmetric full duplex

Some manufacturers have resorted to what is called asymmetric full duplex working on two wire telephone lines. Asymmetric working is a full duplex working system but the data rates in opposite directions are different. The typical data rates used in such a system are 1200 baud in the forward direction and 75 baud in the reverse direction. This is possible on two wire telephone lines because the slower rate of 75 baud requires less bandwidth than a second 1200 baud channel. The advantage of such a system is that it allows limited duplex communication between DTEs for such things as message acknowledgement and error correction.

(d) Throughput efficiency

The *throughput efficiency* is defined as the ratio of the time spent transmitting data to the total time it takes to send a block of data and receive its acknowledgement. Throughput efficiency is dependent on many variables, and I can only give you an example as to what you can expect in a practical case.

Example

In this example, it is assumed that
(1) The data blocks used take 1 s to transmit.
(2) The propagation delay is 3 ms.
(3) The modem turnaround time is 250 ms.
The total time to send a data block and to receive acknowledgement can be calculated as follows:

Modem turnaround time	250 ms
Block transmission time	1000 ms
Modem delay	10 ms
Propagation delay	3 ms
Receiving terminal reaction time	2 ms
Modem turnaround time	250 ms
ACK transmission time	50 ms
Modem delay	10 ms
Propagation delay	3 ms
Transmitting terminal reaction time	2 ms
Total transmission time	1580 ms

$$\text{Throughput efficiency} = \frac{1000}{1580} \times 100 = 63\%$$

2.4 INTERFACES SIMILAR TO RS232

2.4.1 CCITT V24 interface

The CCITT V24 interface is almost identical to RS232. Equipment compatible with RS232 will almost always interface with CCITT V24. However, certain signals have different names. One such example is the 'clear to send' signal; this is known as the 'ready for sending' signal in CCITT terminology. A list of the equivalency of the interchange circuits is given in Fig. 2.9.

2.4.2 CCITT V28 interface

The CCITT V28 interface is virtually identical to RS232C. It differs from RS232C in that it specifies slightly faster rise and fall times through the ± 3 V transition region for data and interchange circuits. For V28, the transition time should not exceed the smaller of either 1 ms or 3% of the bit period. For

	EIA RS-232-C		CCITT RECOMMENDATION V.24
AB	SIGNAL GROUND OR COMMON RET.	102	SIGNAL GROUND OR COMMON RET.
		102a	DTE COMMON RETURN
		102b	DCE COMMON RETURN
CE	RING INDICATOR	125	CALLING INDICATOR
CD	DATA TERMINAL READY	108/2	DATA TERMINAL READY
CC	DATA SET READY	107	DATA SET READY
BA	TRANSMITTED DATA	103	TRANSMITTED DATA
BB	RECEIVED DATA	104	RECEIVED DATA
DA	TRANSMITTER SIGNAL ELEMENT TIMING (DTE SOURCE)	113	TRANSMITTER SIGNAL ELEMENT TIMING (DTE SOURCE)
DB	TRANSMITTER SIGNAL ELEMENT TIMING (DCE SOURCE)	114	TRANSMITTER SIGNAL ELEMENT TIMING (DCE SOURCE)
DD	RECEIVER SIGNAL ELEMENT TIMING	115	RECEIVER SIGNAL ELEMENT TIMING (DCE SOURCE)
CA	REQUEST TO SEND	105	REQUEST TO SEND
CB	CLEAR TO SEND	106	READY FOR SENDING
CF	RECEIVED LINE SIGNAL DETECTOR	109	DATA CHANNEL RECEIVED LINE SIGNAL DETECTOR
CG	SIGNAL QUALITY DETECTOR	110	DATA SIGNAL QUALITY DETECTOR
		126	SELECT TRANSMIT FREQUENCY
CH	DATA SIGNAL RATE SELECTOR (DTE SOURCE)	111	DATA SIGNALLING RATE SELECTOR (DTE SOURCE)
CI	DATA SIGNAL RATE SELECTOR (DCE SOURCE)	112	DATA SIGNALLING RATE SELECTOR (DCE SOURCE)
SBA	SECONDARY TRANSMITTED DATA	118	TRANSMITTED BACKWARD CHANNEL DATA
SBB	SECONDARY RECEIVED DATA	119	RECEIVED BACKWARD CHANNEL DATA
SCA	SECONDARY REQUEST TO SEND	120	TRANSMIT BACKWARD CHANNEL LINE SIGNAL
SCB	SECONDARY CLEAR TO SEND	121	BACKWARD CHANNEL READY
SCF	SECONDARY RECEIVED LINE SIGNAL DETECTOR	122	BACKWARD CHANNEL RECEIVED LINE SIGNAL DETECTOR
		141	LOCAL LOOPBACK
		140	LOOPBACK/MAINTENANCE TEST
		142	TEST INDICATOR
		116	SELECT STANDBY
		117	STANDBY INDICATOR

Fig. 2.9 Interchangeability of circuits.

RS232C, the transition time should not exceed the smaller of either 1 ms or 4% of the bit period. The main properties are summarised in Fig. 2.10(a).

2.4.3   CCITT V10, CCITT X26, RS423A interfaces

CCITT V10, CCITT X26 and RS423A interfaces are also similar and generally compatible with RS232C. They were designed for integrated circuit technology. These interfaces also specify the electrical characteristics of the generators and receivers and give guidance with respect to the interconnecting cable. These interfaces allow faster signalling rates (up to 300 kbps) and

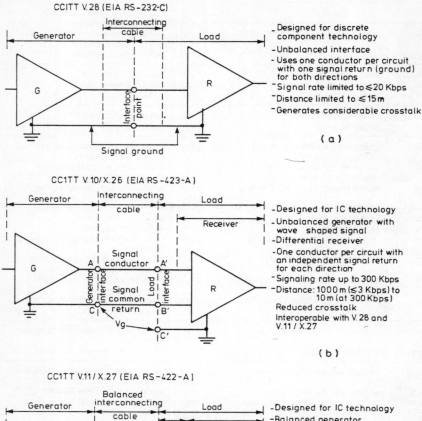

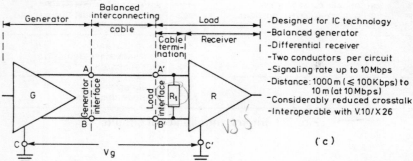

Fig. 2.10 Comparison of electrical characteristics.

longer cable connections. The main differences to RS232C are given in Fig. 2.10(b).

2.4.4   CCITT V11, CCITT X27, RS422A interfaces

CCITT V11, CCITT X27 and RS422A are also similar and generally compatible with RS232C. These interfaces were also designed for integrated technology. The generator and receiver characteristics are also specified. The interfaces feature balanced interconnecting cables. Balanced circuits have a lower capacitance per unit length than unbalanced circuits and therefore degrade high frequency signals less. A balanced circuit comprises a twisted pair of wires, neither of which is earthed. The two leads – known as the A and B wires – carry equal but opposite currents which tend to cancel its magnetic field and reduce interference to other interchange circuits. External interference sources induce equal but opposing voltages into the twisted pair causing a cancellation effect. Hence, balanced circuits are less prone to external interference, and cause less interference to external circuits than an unshielded unbalanced circuit. A pictorial difference of these circuits can be found by examining Fig. 2.10(a) and (c). Data rates up to 10 Mbps can be used in the above interfaces. The main differences to RS232C are shown in Fig. 2.10(c).

2.5 CCITT X21 DIGITAL INTERFACE

The CCITT X21 digital interface (see Fig. 2.11) is designed for compatibility

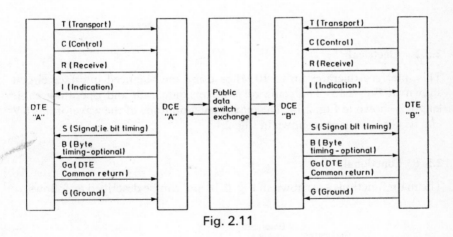

Fig. 2.11

between the customer's computer and/or data terminating equipment (DTE) and the data carrier equipment (DCE) which will carry the digital signals into a public carrier's switched digital exchange for connection to a remote DCE and DTE. It is important because this interface caters for the direct transmission of digital signals from one computer site to another site through public exchange lines.

The standard was first proposed in 1969 and approved in 1976. This standard specifies how the customer's computer or data terminal equipment sets up and clears calls by exchanging signals with the data circuit terminating equipment. The X21 is a long and complicated document with references to other long and complicated documents so I will only pick out the more important aspects of this interface. The description of this interface will be carried out under the four headings used previously, namely, mechanical, electrical, functional and procedural.

2.5.1 Mechanical

The interface uses a 15 pin connector (Fig. 2.12) but not all the pins are used. The pin pair assignments have been carefully chosen to allow either the DTE or DCE work alternative standards.

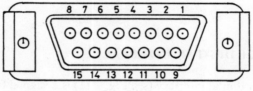

Fig. 2.12

2.5.2 Electrical

This interface operates up to 10 Mbps using the balanced interface circuit shown in Fig. 2.13. The trade off between data rate and operating cable length is shown in Fig. 2.14. The maximum amplitude of the waveform is 6 V and its general shape is shown in Fig. 2.15.

2.5.3 Functional

The main functions are shown in Fig. 2.16 and can be described as follows:

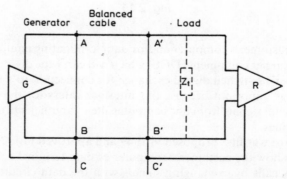

Fig. 2.13 X21 equivalent circuit.

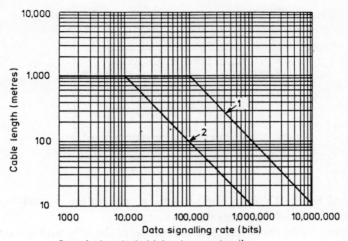

Curve1: terminated interchange circuit
Curve2: unterminated interchange circuit

Fig. 2.14 X21 data signalling rate v cable length for balanced interchange circuit.

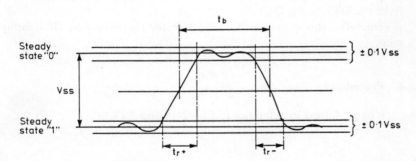

t_b = nominal duration of the test signal element
for $t_b \geqslant 200\,ns$, $t_r \leqslant 0.1\,t_b$
for $t_b < 200\,ns$, $t_r \leqslant 20\,ns$

Fig. 2.15 X21 generator dynamic balance and rise-time measurement.

(1) *T* (*transport*) – this line is used to transmit data from the DTE to the DCE.
(2) *C* (*control*) – this line is used for transmitting control information from the DTE to the DCE.
(3) *R* (*receive*) – the DCE uses this line to send data to the DTE.
(4) *I* (*indication*) – the DCE uses this line to transmit control information to the DTE.
(5) *S* (*signal bit timing*) – the signal bit timing line contains a signal stream

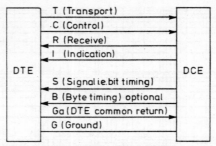

Fig. 2.16 Signal lines used in X21.

emitted by the DCE to provide timing information, so that the DTE knows when each bit interval starts and stops.

(6) *B (byte timing, optional)* – this line provides the user with the option to group the bits into 8 bit frames. If this option is provided, the DTE must begin each character on a frame boundary. If the option is not provided, both DCE and DTE must begin every control sequence with at least two SYN characters to enable the other one to deduce the implied frame boundaries. The SYN character has already been explained under the ASCII transmission code.

(7) *Ga (DTE common ground)* – this is the common return for all signals sent from the DTE to the DCE.

G (ground) – this is the earth connection for the DTE and DCE equipment.

2.5.4 Procedural

This can be explained by reference to Figs 2.16 and 2.17.

(a) Idle state

This is the state when no communication is taking place. Note all four lines, T, C, R, and I, are off, i.e. logic 1.

(b) Communication states

There are ten steps:

(1) DTE wishes to communicate with DCE. For this DTE sends T and C to ON (logic 0).
(2) DCE responds by sending ASCII code '+ + + ...' on line I.
(3) DTE sends destination address on its T line.
(4) DCE responds on its R line by sending *call progress signals* to inform

Step	C	I	Event in telephone analogy	DTE sends on T	DCE sends on R
0	Off	Off	No connection-line idle	T = 1	R = 1
1	On	Off	DTE picks up phone	T = 0	_—
2	On	Off	DCE gives dial tone		R = "+ + + … +"
3	On	Off	DTE dials phone number	T = address	
4	On	Off	Remote phone rings		R = call progress
5	On	On	Remote phone picked up		R = 1
6	On	On	Conversation	T = data	R = data
7	Off	On	DTE says goodbye	T = 0	
8	Off	Off	DCE says goodbye		R = 0
9	Off	Off	DCE hangs up		R = 1
10	Off	Off	DTE hangs up	T = 1	

Fig. 2.17 An example of X21 usage.

DTE of the result of its call. Call progress signals consist of two digit numbers; the first gives the general class of result and the second the details. The general classes include call put through, try again, busy, access barred, etc.

(5) If the destination is obtainable, DCE replies with a 1 on line R.

(6) Two way information transfer is now established via the respective DCEs and the switched equipment. This state continues until either DTE wants to terminate by setting its C line to *off* (logic 1). Having done so, it may not send any more data, but it must be prepared to continue receiving data until the other DTE has finished.

(7) The originating DTE terminates first and turns its C line OFF.

(8) The originating DCE acknowledges this signal by turning its I line to *off*.

(9) When the remote DTE terminates by turning off its C line, the DCE at the originating sets R to 1.

(10) Finally the originating DTE sets T to 1 as an acknowledgement and the interface is back into the idle state, waiting for another call.

The procedure for incoming calls is analogous to that for outgoing calls. If an incoming call and an outgoing call take place simultaneously, known as a *call collision*, the incoming call is cancelled and the outgoing call is put through.

2.6   CENTRONICS INTERFACE

The centronics interface has been chosen for study because it is one of the more popular parallel transmission interfaces for printers and teleprinters. This interface has also been chosen to be the standard printer interface for the MSX series of personal computers.

The important characteristics of the centronics interface will be considered under the usual headings.

2.6.1   Mechanical

The mechanical aspects pertain to the points of demarcation, usually the pluggable connector. The Centronics printer connector is shown in Fig. 2.18. The connector is a 36 pin female connector designated as Amphenol 57-40 360, Centronics P/N 31 310 012-1016, or equivalent. The cable connector that feeds into the printer uses Amphenol 57-30 360 or equivalent. Some printers do not use this connector but use a 44 pin edge connector (Fig. 2.19). This edge connector is known as Centronics no. 3 130 037-1001. It features a key slot between pins 13 and 14 to ensure that the connection can only be made in one orientation.

Figure 2.20 shows the pin connections for the more popular series of Centronics printer interfaces but not all printers (including Centronics printers) are wired for the full list. You should also be aware that some printers use some auxiliary pins for different purposes. The list I have given you is the more general one but you should always check your printer interface against your manual if available. The purpose of each circuit is briefly explained in Fig. 2.20. Functions such as FAULT with a line above the function are read as BAR FAULT or NOT FAULT. They use a logic 1 to indicate the NOT FAULT condition. The recommended cable length is less than 3 m when the standard printer interface is used.

2.6.2   Electrical

Data is transmitted in the parallel format. Eight bits are used but the printer

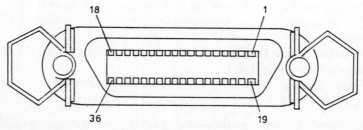

Fig. 2.18 36-pin female connector (Centronics P/N 31310012-1016) or Amphonol 57-40360.

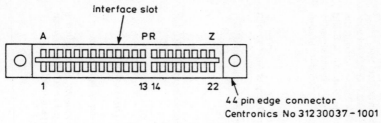

Fig. 2.19

does not read them until it receives a strobe signal to read them. The interface circuit specifications are as follows.

(a) Logic levels

Logic levels are shown in Fig. 2.21. A logic 1 (or high) is defined as a voltage in the range of + 2.4 V to + 5 V. It must not exceed a peak positive voltage of 5.5 V. A logic 0 (or low) is defined as a voltage in the range of 0.0 V to + 0.4 V. It must not exceed a peak negative voltage of − 0.5 V. These logic signal levels are often referred to as TTL type logic signals.

(b) Current requirements

There is also a current requirement in addition to the voltage levels given above. This is that both the sending device and the receiving device (printer) must be capable of providing (sourcing) a current of 0.320 mA when sending logic 1 and absorbing (sinking) a current up to 14 mA when sending logic 0.

(c) Line terminations

The printer interface terminates each INPUT DATA line (D1–D8) with an electrical resistor of 1000 ohms to + 5 V. The control lines NOT DATA STROBE and NOT INPUT PRIME are also connected via 470 ohms resistors to + 5 V. In practice, this means that the ten lines mentioned above are always set to logic 1 by the printer and that it is up to the driving device or computer interface to drag these logic levels down to logic 0 when required.

Data transmission rate varies according to the type of printer being used but transmission rates of up to 100 000 characters per second are possible.

2.6.3 Functional

The function of each circuit is to enable communication between the source or host device (computer) and the printer. Signals sent by the host are 'host generated' and those sent by the printer are 'printer generated'. The timing or duration times of the signals used in this list are those quoted for the Centronics HB series. They vary with different types of printers. I have included a

SIGNAL NAME	INTERFACE CONN.	INTERFACE SLOT	SOURCE	DESCRIPTION
(DATA STROBE)	Pin 1, 19	Pins 21, Y	Input Device	A 1.0 μs pulse (min.) used to clock data from the processor to the printer logic.
DATA 1	2, 20	18, V	Input Device	Input data levels. A high represents a binary ONE, a low represents a ZERO. All printable characters (i.e., codes having a ONE in DATA 6 or DATA 7) are stored in the printer buffer. Control characters (i.e., codes having a ZERO in both DATA 6 and DATA 7), are used to specify special control functions. These codes are not stored in the buffer except when they specify a print command and are preceded by at least one printable character in that line.
DATA 2	3, 21	16, T	Input Device	
DATA 3	4, 22	17, U	Input Device	
DATA 4	5, 23	20, X	Input Device	
DATA 5	6, 24	15, S	Input Device	
DATA 6	7, 25	11, N	Input Device	
DATA 7	8, 26	19, W	Input Device	
DATA 8	9, 27	12, P	Input Device	
ACKNLG	10, 28	22, T	Printer	Acknowledge pulse indicates the input of a character into memory or the end of a functional operation.
BUSY	11, 29	3, C	Printer	A level indicating that the printer cannot receive data. For conditions causing BUSY, refer to Busy Condition Timing Table.
PE	12	9	Printer	A level indicating that the printer is out of paper.
SLCT	13	F	Printer	A level indicating that the printer is selected.
±0V	14	7	Printer	Signal ground (Formerly SS signal, older version)
OSCXT	15	H	Printer	A 100 kHz signal (Models 101, 101A, 102A, 101S) or 100-200 kHz signal (All other models).
±0V	16	A	Printer	Signal ground
Chassis Gnd	17	—	Printer	Frame ground
+5V	18	13	Printer	+5 Volt power bus
(INPUT PRIME)	31, 30	L, 10	Input Device	A level which clears the printer buffer and initialises the logic. (Not in 101).
FAULT	32	M	Printer	A level that indicates a printer fault condition such as paper empty, light detect, or a deselect condition. (Not in 101).
Line Count Pulse	34, 35	2, D		Both sides of the line count switch appear at the interface connector. This switch is opened and closed during each line feed operation. A level delivered to the switch would be pulsed off and on each time a line feed operation is performed. (Series 300 and 500 except 306SC, 503).
Not used	36			

NOTES: 1. Second pin number indicates twisted pair return (±0V).

Fig. 2.20 Pins and slot connection for Centronics printer.

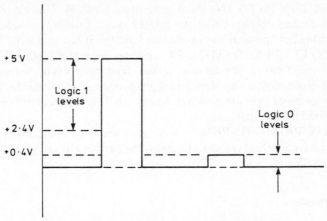

Fig. 2.21 Logic level for Centronics printer.

list of other timings in Fig. 2.24 but ignore that figure temporarily. The functions of the individual circuits are as follows:

(1) DATA1–DATA8 (host generated) [pins 2–9]. Data lines 1 through 8 carry ASCII character and control code information plus graphic image data. Data is true when high (logic 1).

(2) DATA STROBE (STB – host generated) [pin 1]. This negative going pulse transfers data from the host into the electronics of the printer. The pulse duration of the strobe signal must be at least $0.5\,\mu s$ for the Centronics HB series, or at least $1\,\mu s$ for other printers.

(3) ACKNOWLEDGE (ACKNLG – printer generated) [pin 10]. This negative going pulse ($18\,\mu s$) indicates that the printer has processed the latest byte of data. The acknowledge signal is also sent to the host under the following conditions: (a) after power-up and ON LINE, (b) after input prime input.

(4) BUSY (printer generated) [pin 11]. This positive going signal indicates that the printer cannot accept new data. The busy signal is active under these conditions: printer deselected (OFF LINE), leading edge of input prime signal and buffer full condition.

(5) SELECT (SLCT – printer generated) [pin 13]. This positive signal indicates that the printer is ON LINE and ready to accept data (if not busy). SELECT is inactive under the following conditions: when the printer is OFF LINE, the printer is remotely deselected (DC3 code), input prime signal and paper end condition (out of paper).

(6) PAPER END (PE – printer generated) [pin 12]. This positive going signal indicates an out of paper condition which deselects the printer (unless switch is in CUT SHEET position). After replenishing paper, the printer must be selected by pressing ON LINE.

(7) FAULT (FAULT – printer generated) [pin 32]. This is a negative going signal which indicates printer OFF LINE or out of paper (PE).

(8) SELECT IN (SLCT IN – host generated) [pin 36]. This allows remote selection and deselection of the printer. Most printers provide a switch to enable the operator to disable this function if not required.

(9) AUTO LINE FEED (AUTO LF – printer generated) [pin 14]. This low level signal causes an automatic line feed after each carriage return (CR). Note most computers and word processors provide this function. Most printers provide a switch to disable this function if it is already provided by the host.

(10) INPUT PRIME (INPRM – host generated) [pin 31]. This negative going signal (50 μs) resets (initialises) the printer circuitry and clears the print buffer.

2.6.4 Procedural

This is best explained by reference to the case in Fig. 2.22 where a computer wishes to print out data through a Centronics interface printer. I shall assume that the printer and the computer are compatible for interfacing.

(1) After the printer is switched on, it sends a positive signal (SLCT) to indicate to the computer that it is ON LINE. (I shall assume that there is already paper in the printer and that remote selection of the printer is unnecessary.)

(2) The computer acknowledges this before printing by sending a negative going signal INPUT PRIME to initialise the printer circuitry and to clear the print buffer.

(3) The printer replies with an ACKNOWLEDGE signal to indicate that it is ready for data.

(4) The computer then puts its data bits for a character on the input data

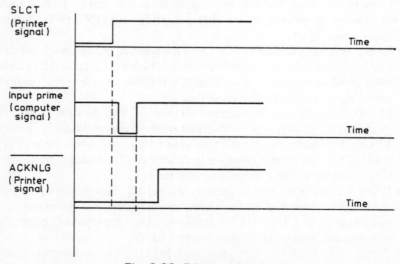

Fig. 2.22 Printer selection.

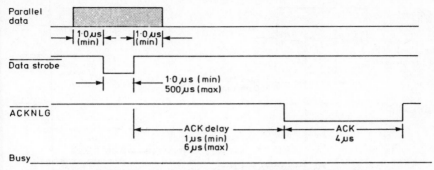

Fig. 2.23 Normal timing procedure for data transfer.

lines (see Fig. 2.23). This data is transmitted across to the printer but the printer does not read these signals because the electrical state of these data lines has not yet reached a steady state. This steady state is reached approximately 1 μs later when the computer sends a strobe signal to instruct the printer to read the information on the data lines. The printer then reads the data but the computer must hold the data lines steady for at least another microsecond after the end of the strobe signal to enable the printer to complete reading the data.

(5) After reading the character data, the printer is allowed up to 6 μs to decide if the data is valid. If the data is valid, then it must send an ACKNOWLEDGE signal back to computer.

(6) The receipt of the ACKNOWLEDGE signal from the printer indicates to the computer that its last character has been received and that it can send another character. Items (4), (5) and (6) are then repeated until all the data has been sent.

(7) The printer is sometimes unable to respond to the strobe signal given in item (4). The reason for this lack of response can be due to one or more reasons; the printer may have a fault, it may be out of paper, its buffer may be full and it can accept no more information, or the printer may be off line. Each of these conditions can be signalled to the computer. If the printer is busy (Fig. 2.24) the data on the lines will be maintained until the printer is ready to process it.

(8) The timing signal I have given you in Fig. 2.23 is only representative of some Centronics type of printers. The actual signal timing varies according to the particular printer even for the same manufacturer and I have included a representative sample (see Fig. 2.25) for your reference. The information given above should be enough to enable you to understand your printer manual and to allow you to connect a Centronics type printer to a personal computer successfully.

2.7 IEEE448 COMMUNICATIONS INTERFACE

The IEEE448 communications interface bus (Fig. 2.26) has been chosen for

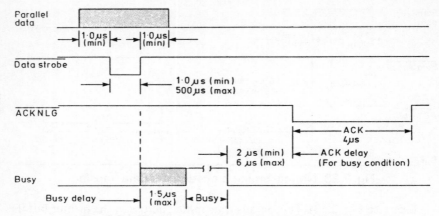

Fig. 2.24 Timing procedure when printer is busy.

investigation because it is the dominant control interface used for communications between computers and their peripherals. This interface is also known as the general purpose interface bus (GPIB) and the Hewlett Packard interface bus (HPIB).

The interface was originally patented by the Hewlett Packard company and used for computer control of their measuring instruments and manufacturing processes. It was subsequently licensed to other developers of general purpose interface bus systems. The Institute of Electrical and Electronic Engineers adopted this interface standard as IEEE448 in 1975 and updated it in 1978.

2.7.1 Bus structure

The main objective of the IEEE448 interface is to provide a transparent communications channel which allows the equipment of different manufacturers to be interconnected in a single network. The peripheral equipment connected to the bus is classified as listeners (receivers of information), talkers (sources of information), controllers (devices which control data transfer) or any combination of these.

The system also has the following defined constraints:

(1) No more than fifteen devices can be interconnected by a single contiguous bus.
(2) Total transmission length is not to exceed 20 m, or 2 m times the number of devices, whichever is less.
(3) All data exchange is to be digital.
(4) Data rate through any signal line must be less than, or equal to 1 Mbit/s.

2.7.2 Bus signals

There are three sets of bus signals (Fig. 2.26) which comprise the sixteen lines in the system. The bidirectional *data* bus contains the eight lines used to transfer data. Control of the data is exercised by the three wire *handshaking* bus. Other control signals are transmitted on the general interface *management* bus. The latter consists of five lines.

2.7.3 Mechanical

The IEEE448 standard specifies the dimensions (Fig. 2.27), the actual pin locations (Fig. 2.28), voltage rating (200 V), current rating (5 amps per contact) and the general composition of the connector.

2.7.4 Electrical

Specifications for the voltage levels associated with the logic signals used in reception are shown in Fig. 2.29. The maximum speed of data transmission is limited to 1 Mbit/s per signal line, but each line may be operated simultaneously. This means that in the case of eight bit characters, character transmission rates of 1 million characters per second are possible.

2.7.5 Functional

A list of the signal circuits has been introduced in Fig. 2.28. The purpose function of each signal circuit will now be explained.

(1) The data input/output lines (DIO1–DIO8). These are the message lines for carrying data; eight bits of data (one per line) forming a character byte are transmitted simultaneously on these lines. Characters are transmitted sequentially. Data transmitted in such a manner is said to be transmitted in a bit-parallel, byte serial form. Data is transmitted asynchronous and generally bidirectional. These lines carry either data or address information, depending on the condition of the ATN line.

(2) Data valid line (DAV). One of the three handshake lines used to indicate availability and validity of information on the DIO lines. DAV indicates to the receiving peripherals that data is available on the DIO lines.

(3) Not ready for data line (NRFD). Another handshake line used to indicate that all devices are or are not ready to accept data. This line cannot be set to the 'READY FOR DATA' mode until all the listening devices on the bus are ready for data.

(4) Not data accepted line (NDAC). The final handshake line to indicate the acceptance of data by all listening devices. This line will not signal 'DATA ACCEPTED' until all the listening devices have accepted the data.

(5) Attention line (ATN). One of five bus management lines used to specify how data on the data lines are to be interpreted and which devices must respond to the data. When ATN is true, the DIO1–8 lines carry addresses or commands. When false, they carry data. (Controller driven.)

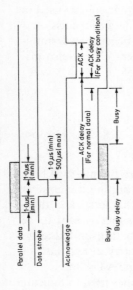

Parallel data
Data strobe
Acknowledge
Busy

1.0 μs (min)
1.0 μs (min)
1.0 μs (min) 500 μs (max)

ACK delay (For normal data)
ACK delay (For busy condition)
ACK
Busy delay
Busy

	101/101A/101S	101AL	102A	102AL	103	104	301	306	306C	306SC
ACK DELAY	7 usec. 4 usec.	2.5–10 usec. 2.5–5.0 usec.	7 usec. 4 usec.	2.5–10 usec. 2.5–5.0 usec.	2.5–10 usec. 2.5–5.0 usec.	2.5–10 usec. 2.5–5.0 usec.	2.5–10 usec. 2.5–5.0 usec.	2.5–10 usec. 2.5–5.0 usec.	2.5–10 usec. 2.5–5.0 usec.	2.5–10 usec. 2.5–5.0 usec.
NORMAL DATA INPUT TIMING										
BUSY DELAY	0	0–1.5 usec.	0	0–1.5 usec.	0–1.5 usec.	0–1.5 usec.	0–1.5 usec.	0–1.5 usec.	0–1.5 usec.	0–1.5 usec.
ACK DELAY	0	0–10 usec.	0	0–10 usec.	0–10 usec.	0–10 usec.	0–10 usec.	0–10 usec.	0–10 usec.	0–10 usec.
ACK	4 usec.	2.5–5.0 usec.	4 usec.	2.5–5.0 usec.	2.5–5.0 usec.	2.5–5.0 usec.	2.5–5.0 usec.	2.5–5.0 usec.	2.5–5.0 usec.	2.5–5.0 usec.
BUSY CONDITION TIMING										
BUSY DURATION:										
Line Feed	75–105 msec.	75–105 msec.	75–105 msec.	16 msec. (single LF) 75–105 msec. (multiple LF)	16 msec. (single LF) 51 msec. (double LF) 25–75 msec. (multiple LF)	10 msec. (single LF) 25 msec. (double LF) 70–77 msec. (multiple LF)	70–100 msec.	75–105 msec.	75–105 msec. (single LF)	35–50 msec.
Vertical Tab (1-inch)	300–310 msec.	300–310 msec.	300–310 msec.	300–310 msec.	125 msec.	125 msec.	160–200 msec.	300–310 msec.	300–310 msec.	155–170 msec.
Form Feed (11 inches)	3–3.5 sec.	3–3.5 sec.	3–3.5 sec.	3–3.5 sec.	1.4 sec.	1.4 sec.	1.5–2.0 sec.	3–3.5 sec.	3–3.5 sec.	1.40–1.42 sec.
Delete	3 msec.	100–400 usec.	3 msec.	100–400 usec.	160–400 usec.	100–400 usec.	100–400 usec.	100–400 usec.	100–400 usec.	100–400 usec.
Bell	2 sec.	0	2 sec.	0	0	0	0	0	0	0
Select	3 msec.	100–400 usec.	3 msec.	100–400 usec.	100–400 usec.	100–400 usec.	100–400 usec.	100–400 usec.	100–400 usec.	100–400 usec.
Deselect	Until printer is selected	Until printer is selected	Until printer is selected	Until printer is selected	Until printer is selected	Until printer is selected	Until printer is selected	Until printer is selected	Until printer is selected	Until printer is selected
Print Command	6 msec./char plus 75–105 msec. LF	6 msec./char plus 75–105 msec. LF	470–500 msec. (total)	410–415 msec. (total)	6 msec./char plus 16 msec. LF	300 msec.	6 msec./char plus 70–100 msec. LF	8.4 msec./char plus 75–105 msec. LF	10/8.4/6.6/6.0 msec./char (10/12/15/16.5 cpl)	8.4 msec./char plus 35–50
(Return time-no busy)	(240 msec. max)	(240 msec. max)	(0)	(0)	(0)	(0)	(270 msec. max)	(270 msec. max)	(270 msec. max)	(270 msec. max)

NORMAL DATA INPUT TIMING

BUSY CONDITION TIMING

	500	501	503	588	500D	501D	588D	700	701
ACK DELAY	2.5–10 usec. 2.5–5.0 usec.	2.5–10 usec. 2.5–5.0 usec.	2.5–10 usec. 2.5–5.0 usec.	2.5–10 usec. 2.5–5.0 usec.	2.5–10 usec. 2.5–5.0 usec.	2.5–10 usec. 2.5–5.0 usec.	2.5–10 usec. 2.5–5.0 usec.	2.5–10 usec. 2.5–5.0 usec.	2.5–10 usec. 2.5–5.0 usec.
BUSY DELAY	0–1.5 usec.	0–1.5 usec.	0–1.5 usec.	0–1.5 usec.	0–1.5 usec.	0–1.5 usec.	0–1.5 usec.	0–1.5 usec.	0–1.5 usec.
ACK DELAY	0–10 usec.	0–10 usec.	0–10 usec.	0–10 usec.	0–10 usec.	0–10 usec.	0–10 usec.	0–10 usec.	0–10 usec.
ACK	2.5–5.0 usec.	2.5–5.0 usec.	2.5–5.0 usec.	2.5–5.0 usec.	2.5–5.0 usec.	2.5–5.0 usec.	2.5–5.0 usec.	2.5–5.0 usec.	2.5–5.0 usec.
BUSY DURATION: Line Feed	75–105 msec.	70–100 msec.	16 msec. (single LF) 51 msec. (double LF) 25–75 msec. (multiple LF)	75–105 msec.	20 msec.	20 msec.	20 msec.	75–105 msec.	75–105 msec.
Vertical Tab (1-inch) Form feed (11-inches)	300–310 msec.	160–200 msec.	125 msec.	300–310 msec.	20 msec.	20 msec.	20 msec.	240–270 msec.	240–270 msec.
Delete	3–3.5 sec.	1.5–2.0 sec.	1.4 sec.	3–3.5 sec.	20 msec.	20 msec.	20 msec.	2.07–2.11 sec.	2.07–2.11 sec.
Bell	100–400 usec.	100–400 usec.	160–400 usec.	100–400 usec.	100–400 usec.	100–400 usec.	100–400 usec.	100–400 usec.	100–400 usec.
Select*	0	0	0	0	0	0	0	0	0
Deselect	100–400 usec.	100–400 usec.	100–400 usec.	100–400 usec.	100–400 usec.	100–400 usec.	100–400 usec.	100–400 usec.	100–400 usec.
Print Command	Until printer is selected 8.4 msec./char plus 75–105 msec. LF	Until printer is selected 6 msec./char plus 70–100 msec. LF	Until printer is selected 6 msec./char plus 16 msec. LF	Until printer is selected 11.3 msec./char plus 75–105 msec. LF	Until printer is selected 8.4/7 msec./char (10/12 cpi) .20 msec. LF	Until printer is selected 6 msec./char 20 msec. LF	Until printer is selected 11.3/9.4/6.9 msec./char (10/12/16.5 cpi) .20 msec. LF	Until printer is selected 16.7 msec./char	Until printer is selected 16.7 msec./char
(Return time-no-busy)	(400 msec. max)	(400 msec. max)	(0)	(400 msec. max)	(400 msec. max)	(400 msec. max)	(400 msec. max)	2.2 sec (max)	(0)

*No. busy, if inhibit prime on select option is used.

Fig. 2.25 Some interface timings for Centronics printers.

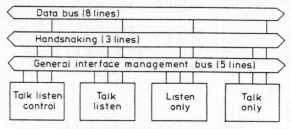

Fig. 2.26 IEEE448 bus system.

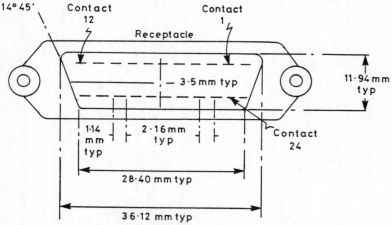

Fig. 2.27 Device connector mounting.

Contact	Signal Line	Contact	Signal Line
1	DIO1	13	DIO5
2	DIO2	14	DIO6
3	DIO3	15	DIO7
4	DIO4	16	DIO8
5	EOI	17	REN
6	DAV	18	Gnd. (6)
7	NRFD	19	Gnd. (7)
8	NDAC	20	Gnd. (8)
9	IFC	21	Gnd. (9)
10	SRQ	22	Gnd. (10)
11	ATN	23	Gnd. (11)
12	SHIELD	24	Gnd. LOGIC

NOTE: Gnd. (*n*) refers to the signal ground return of the referenced contact.

Fig. 2.28 IEEE448 connector pin assignments.

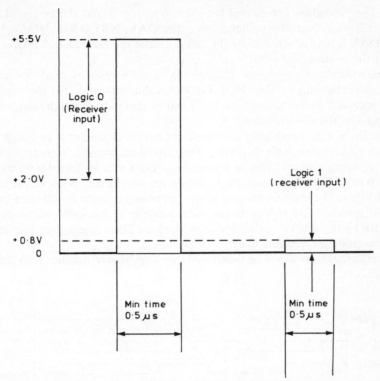

Fig. 2.29 Electrical levels for IEEE448 logic signals.

(6) Interface clear line (IFC). A bus management line which is used to place the interface system in a known quiescent state. All interconnected devices contain some portions of the interface system. IFC puts talkers, listeners into their idle states. (Controller driven.)

(7) Service request line (SRQ). A bus management line used by a device to indicate a need for service and to request an interrupt of the current events sequence.

(8) Remote enable line (REN). This management line, in conjunction with other messages, selects between two alternate sources of device programming data. (Example: front panel control or interface control.) (Controller driven.)

(9) End or identify line (EOI). The final management line used to indicate the end of multiple byte transfer sequences or with ATN to perform a parallel polling sequence.

2.7.6 Procedural

When data is transferred from a source to one or more acceptors, a handshaking procedure is utilised to ensure that the transfer is performed properly. The procedure is repeated for each byte transferred. Three signal lines (Fig. 2.30) are used for the handshake: the DAV, NRFD and NDAC lines. The DAV line is controlled by the talker, while the NRFD and NDAC are under the control of the listeners.

The handshake procedure ensures that each listener is ready to accept data, that the data on the DIO1–DIO8 is valid data and that the data has been accepted by all the listeners. Data will be sent only as rapidly as it can be accepted by the slowest listener.

The three wire handshake has three important characteristics which give the interface system wide flexibility. First, the data transfer is asynchronous, thus avoiding inherent timing restrictions. Data can be transferred at any rate up to 1 Mbps that is suitable to the devices on the bus. Second, the handshake allows the interconnection of devices which operate at different input/output speeds. Data is transferred automatically at the speed which can be handled by the slowest active device on the bus. Third, more than one device can accept data simultaneously.

A handshake cycle will be illustrated in a step by step manner with the aid of Fig. 2.30.

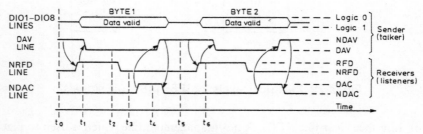

Fig. 2.30 IEEE448 handshake timing diagram.

(1) At time t_0, shortly after switch on, the sender sets its handshake line to the NDAV position, the receivers set their handshake lines to the NRFD and NDAC positions.
(2) At time t_1 the sender and the receivers have had time to settle down. The sender loads its data lines with data and the receivers indicate that they are in a position to receive data by setting their handshake line to the RFD position.
(3) At time t_2 the sender, sensing the RFD position of the receivers' handshake line, sets its handshake line to the DAV position to indicate that the data on the data lines (DIO1–DIO8) is valid. The receivers receive the data byte (eight bits simultaneously).
(4) At time t_3 the receivers indicate that they are busy by setting the NRFD position.
(5) At time t_4 the receivers acknowledge receipt of the byte.
(6) At time t_5 the sender notes the acknowledgement by setting its hand-

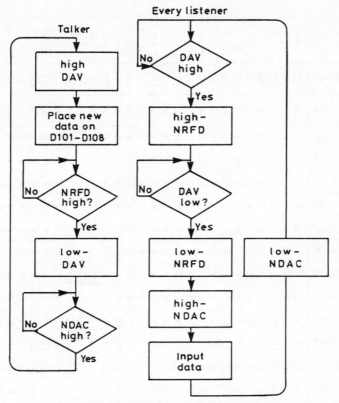

Fig. 2.31 Flowcharts of bus operations.

shake line to the NDAV position and prepares to reset the data lines for the next byte.

(7) At time t_6 the receivers indicate that they are ready to receive another byte and the whole handshake sequence is repeated again and again until only the last byte remains to be sent. In transmitting the last byte, the sender labels it in a data transfer with a monitor bit. When EOI is set to logic 1, the listeners know that the transfer has been completed.

A flowchart of the bus operations is shown in Fig. 2.31. This flowchart should now be self-explanatory.

2.7.7 Controller communications

Communications between a controller and the listeners is quite similar to that used by the talker, but the controller is capable of more activities. A list of possible messages and commands is shown in the table in Fig. 2.32.

A controller can disable the local controls on a talker/listener with the REN signal. When the REN signal is asserted (logic 1), remote control is in

| | | Bus Signal Line(s) and Coding That Assert Message True | | | | | | | | | | | | | | | | | | |
| | | Data I/O | | | | | | | | Handshake | | | Bus Management | | | | | | | |
Mnemonic	Message Name	DIO8	DIO7	DIO6	DIO5	DIO4	DIO3	DIO2	DIO1	DAV	NRFD	NDAC	ATN	EOI	SRQ	IFC	REN	Message Type	Message Class	Notes
ACG	Addressed Command Group	X	0	0	0	X	X	X	X	X	X	X	1	X	X	X	X	M	AC	10
ATN	Attention	X	X	X	X	X	X	X	X	X	X	X	1	X	X	X	X	U	UC	—
DAB	Data Byte	D8	D7	D6	D5	D4	D3	D2	D1	1	X	X	0	X	X	X	X	M	DD	1,9
DAC	Data Accepted	X	X	X	X	X	X	X	X	X	X	X	X	X	X	X	X	U	HS	—
DCL	Device Clear	X	0	0	1	0	1	0	0	X	X	X	1	X	X	X	X	M	UC	10
END	End	X	X	X	X	X	X	X	X	X	X	X	0	1	X	X	X	U	ST	9,11
EOS	End of String	E8	E7	E6	E5	E4	E3	E2	E1	X	X	X	0	X	X	X	X	M	DD	2,9
GET	Group Execute Trigger	X	0	0	0	1	0	0	0	X	X	X	1	X	X	X	X	M	AC	10
GTL	Go To Local	X	0	0	0	0	0	0	1	X	X	X	1	X	X	X	X	M	AC	10
IDY	Identify	X	X	X	X	X	X	X	X	X	X	X	1	1	X	X	X	U	UC	10,11
IFC	Interface Clear	X	X	X	X	X	X	X	X	X	X	X	X	X	X	1	X	U	UC	—
LAG	Listen Address Group	X	0	1	X	X	X	X	X	X	X	X	1	X	X	X	X	M	AD	10
LLO	Local Lock Out	X	0	0	1	0	0	0	1	X	X	X	1	X	X	X	X	M	UC	10
MLA	My Listen Address	X	0	1	L5	L4	L3	L2	L1	X	X	X	1	X	X	X	X	M	AD	3,10
MTA	My Talk Address	X	1	0	T5	T4	T3	T2	T1	X	X	X	1	X	X	X	X	M	AD	4,10
MSA	My Secondary Address	X	1	1	S5	S4	S3	S2	S1	X	X	X	1	X	X	X	X	M	SE	5,10
NUL	Null Byte	0	0	0	0	0	0	0	0	X	X	X	X	X	X	X	X	M	DD	10
OSA	Other Secondary Address	(OSA = SCG $\wedge$ $\overline{\text{MSA}}$)								X	X	X	1	X	X	X	X	M	SE	10
OTA	Other Talk Address	(OTA = TAG $\wedge$ $\overline{\text{MTA}}$)								X	X	X	1	X	X	X	X	M	AD	10
PCG	Primary Command Group	(PCG = ACG $\vee$ UCG $\vee$ LAG $\vee$ TAG)								X	X	X	1	X	X	X	X	M	—	10
PPC	Parallel Poll Configure	X	0	0	0	0	1	0	1	X	X	X	1	X	X	X	X	M	AC	10
PPE	Parallel Poll Enable	X	1	1	0	S	P3	P2	P1	X	X	X	1	X	X	X	X	M	SE	6,10
PPD	Parallel Poll Disable	X	1	1	1	D4	D3	D2	D1	X	X	X	1	X	X	X	X	M	SE	7,10
PPR1	Parallel Poll Response 1	X	X	X	X	X	X	X	1	X	X	X	1	1	X	X	X	U	ST	—
PPR2	Parallel Poll Response 2	X	X	X	X	X	X	1	X	X	X	X	1	1	X	X	X	U	ST	—
PPR3	Parallel Poll Response 3	X	X	X	X	X	1	X	X	X	X	X	1	1	X	X	X	U	ST	—
PPR4	Parallel Poll Response 4	X	X	X	X	1	X	X	X	X	X	X	1	1	X	X	X	U	ST	—
PPR5	Parallel Poll Response 5	X	X	X	1	X	X	X	X	X	X	X	1	1	X	X	X	U	ST	—
PPR6	Parallel Poll Response 6	X	X	1	X	X	X	X	X	X	X	X	1	1	X	X	X	U	ST	—
PPR7	Parallel Poll Response 7	X	1	X	X	X	X	X	X	X	X	X	1	1	X	X	X	U	ST	—

Mnemonic	Message	DIO8	DIO7	DIO6	DIO5	DIO4	DIO3	DIO2	DIO1	Type	Class	Notes
PPR8	Parallel Poll Response 8	1	X	X	X	X	X	X	X	U	ST	—
PPU	Parallel Poll Unconfigure	X	Ø	Ø	1	Ø	1	Ø	1	M	UC	10
REN	Remote Enable	X	X	X	X	X	X	X	X	U	UC	—
RFD	Ready For Data	X	X	X	X	X	X	X	1	U	HS	9
RQS	Request Service	X	1	X	X	X	X	X	X	U	ST	10
SCG	Secondary Command Group	X	1	1	S	S	S	S	S	M	SE	10
SDC	Selected Device Clear	X	Ø	Ø	Ø	Ø	1	Ø	Ø	M	AC	10
SPD	Serial Poll Disable	X	Ø	Ø	1	1	Ø	Ø	1	M	UC	10
SPE	Serial Poll Enable	X	Ø	Ø	1	1	Ø	Ø	Ø	M	UC	10
SRQ	Service Request	X	X	X	X	X	X	X	X	U	ST	—
STB	Status Byte	S8	X	S6	S5	S4	S3	S2	S1	M	ST	8,9
TCT	Take Control	X	Ø	Ø	Ø	1	Ø	Ø	1	M	AC	10
TAG	Talk Address Group	X	1	Ø	T	T	T	T	T	M	AD	10
UGG	Universal Command Group	X	Ø	Ø	1	X	X	X	X	M	UC	10
UNL	Unlisten	X	Ø	1	1	1	1	1	1	M	AD	10
UNT	Untalk	X	1	Ø	1	1	1	1	1	M	AD	10

Symbols:

Type   U = Uniline message
       M = Multiline message
Class AC = Addressed command
       AD = Address (talk or listen)
       DD = Device dependent
       HS = Handshake
       UC = Universal Command
       SE = Secondary
       ST = Status

Ø = logical zero (HIGH Signal Level)
1 = logical one (LOW Signal Level)
X = don't care (for the coding of a received message)
X = must not drive (for the coding of a transmitted message)

NOTES:

(1) D1–D8 specify the device dependent data bits.

(2) E1–E8 specify the device dependent code used to indicate the EOS message.

(3) L1–L5 specify the device dependent bits of the device's listen address.

(4) T1–T5 specify the device dependent bits of the device's talk address.

(5) S1–S5 specify the device dependent bits of the device's secondary address.

(6) S specifies the sense of the PPR.

S	Response
Ø	
1	

P1–P3 specify the PPR message to be sent when a parallel poll is executed.

P3	P2	P1	PPR Message
Ø	Ø	Ø	PPR1
.	.	.	
.	.	.	
1	1	1	PPR8

(7) D1–D4 specify don't-care bits that must be sent all zeroes, but do not need to be decoded by the receiving device.

(8) S1–S6, S8 specify the device dependent status. (DIO7 is used for the RQS message.)

(9) The true message value must be ignored when received if the LACS is inactive.

(10) The true message value must be ignored when received if the ATN message is false.

(11) Interface protocol specifies that the IDY message is sent true only when the ATN message is sent true, whereas the END message is sent true only when the ATN message is sent false.

Fig. 2.32 Table for remote message coding.

effect. Return to manual control is effected by removing REN (logic 0). The transition in either direction must be carried out within 100 μs.

A controller can also take command of the bus by asserting the ATN lines. When in the command mode, the controller uses data bus lines DIO1–5 to specify a particular address and lines DIO6–7 to issue commands.

The use of the commands shown in Fig. 2.32 is best illustrated by examples. If the controller asserts ATN and outputs on the data lines:

DIO8	DIO7	DIO6	DIO5	DIO4	DIO3	DIO3	DIO1
X	0	1	0	0	0	1	1

It means that device 3 is to listen to its commands. You can verify this by scanning Fig. 2.32 until you come to the mnemonic MLA. Lines DIO7–6 give the command lister, while DIO1–5 give the address 3 in binary.

Similarly, if the controller asserts the ATN line and outputs on the data lines:

DIO8	DIO7	DIO6	DIO5	DIO4	DIO3	DIO2	DIO1
X	1	0	0	0	1	0	1

It means that device 5 is to be the talker. Again you can verify this by the mnemonic MTA in Fig. 2.32. Lines DIO7–6 give the command listen while DIO5–1 give the address 5 in binary.

Some commands (known as universal commands) do not require addressing. One such command shown in Fig. 2.32 is the DCL (device clear) command. If the controller asserts the ATN line and outputs on the data lines:

DIO8	DIO7	DIO6	DIO5	DIO4	DIO3	DIO2	DIO1
X	0	0	1	0	1	0	0

All devices on the bus enter their initialisation sequence thus forcing each device into a known initial state.

To illustrate the use of some of the above bus management commands, consider a system comprising a computer, which acts as both the bus controller and also a talker and a listener, and a number of slave devices which may function as either talkers or listeners. A typical sequence followed by the computer to request one of the slave devices to take a preprogrammed number of readings and return these to the controller could be as follows:

(1) The controller first initialises all the bus interface circuits by asserting the IFC line; this allows the controller to communicate with each device in a reliable way.
(2) The controller then initialises all the slave devices by placing the DCL (device clear bit) pattern on to the data lines and asserting the ATN line. When all the slave devices have completed the handshake procedure for this command byte, the controller knows each device is in a known initialised state.
(3) The controller sets the particular slave device to be a listener and itself to be a talker.

(4) The controller sets the bus into the data mode and transfers a known byte to the selected slave device which, it is assumed, has been pre-programmed to interpret this as a trigger to start taking readings.

(5) The controller resets the status of the slave device and then proceeds to set it up as a talker and, in turn, sets itself up as a listener.

(6) When the slave device has completed taking the preprogrammed number of readings, it proceeds to transfer the readings – one byte at a time – to the controller now acting as a listener on the bus.

(7) On receipt of the set of readings the computer would typically process them and possibly output the results on a display or printer.

The above sequence is only one possible method of controlling the bus for the transfer of data. Other methods exist and these vary according to the manufacturer of a particular system. There are also many integrated circuits designed for use with the IEEE448 interface.

CHAPTER 3
Interface Case Studies

3.0 INTERFACE CASE STUDIES

These case studies are based on computer signals which were measured prior to writing. It should be realised that most computers are obsolescent by the time they go on sale, but the interface principles remain the same for a particular international standard. Therefore, do not worry too much about a particular piece of equipment, concentrate instead on the principles so that you may apply them to your own equipment.

3.1 INTRODUCTION

Before going on to the actual case studies in this section, I would like to refresh your memory concerning the RS232 interface explained in the previous chapter. If you refer back to Fig. 2.1 you will see that the overall communications system from computer A to computer B actually involves three communications systems. These are:

(1) computer A to modem A
(2) modem A to modem B
(3) modem B to computer B.

It follows that if a peripheral has the communication facilities provided by modem A on its computer communications side, the peripheral will be able to communicate with computer A (see Fig. 3.1). This is what some manufacturers mean when RS232 compatibility is claimed for a printer.

Some typewriter/printers possess fuller RS232 compatibility in that they can also be used to reproduce the signalling procedures provided by computer A to modem A. In this case, it is possible for a typewriter/printer con-

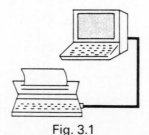

Fig. 3.1

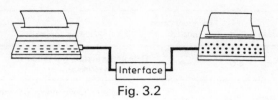

Fig. 3.2

nected in computer A's position to communicate with a similar typewriter/ printer either directly (Fig. 3.2) or indirectly (Fig. 3.3). Communications between teleprinters are usually carried out in the manner shown in Fig. 3.3.

In the two case studies given in this section, I will deal with the system shown in Fig. 3.1 only. I will describe each case study using the method used previously to examine interfaces and protocols, namely, physical, electrical, functional and procedural.

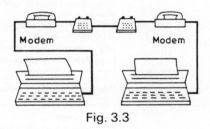

Fig. 3.3

3.2   CASE STUDY 1: RS423, CCITT V10

The first case study concerns the protocol which takes place between a personal computer (BBC model B) and a printer/typewriter (Brother model EP44) when information is transferred from the former to the latter. The computer claims RS423 compatibility, but does not possess the complete RS423 facilities. The printer claims RS232C compatibility but does not possess the complete RS232C facilities.

3.2.1   Physical

The serial port of the BBC computer does not use the recommended 25 pin connector. It uses a standard 5 pin DIN socket (Fig. 3.4). The five pin connections include (1) data in, (2) data out, (3) request to send RTS, (4) clear to send CTS and (5) common signal ground GND.

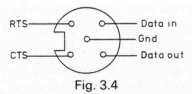

Fig. 3.4

Terminal number	Signal name	Code	EP↔connected device	Function summary	Note
2	Send Data	SD	→	Data line sent from this printer to connected terminal	
3	Receive Data	RD	←	Data line sent from connected terminal to this printer	
4	Request to Send	RS	→	Controls transmission carrier ON: carrier output OFF: carrier stop	Normally ON in the terminal mode
5	Clear to Send	CS	←	Controls data transmission ON: data transmission possible OFF: data transmission not possible	
6	Data set Ready	DR	←	Indicates condition of connected device ON: transmission/reception possible at connected device OFF: transmission/reception not possible at connected device	ON when cable is not connected
7	Signal Ground	SG	↔	Provides basic ground potential	
8	Carrier Detect	CD	←	Detects carrier ON: receiving access signal OFF: not receiving access signal	ON when cable is not connected
20	External Ready	ER	→	Indicates condition of this printer ON: printer preparation completed OFF: printer preparation not completed	Enables on/off setting selection. ON unless otherwise specified.

ON: +V
OFF: −V

Fig. 3.5 Connector and pin arrangement.

The serial port of the printer EP44 (Fig. 3.5) uses the standard 25 pin RS232C connector. Only eight wires are connected to this socket: seven signal lines and a common signal return. This is not the full complement of RS232 signals. The connecting cable between the two devices for data transferral from the computer to the printer is shown in Fig. 3.6.

3.2.2 Electrical

The signal waveforms are compatible for interface operation provided the signalling rates and cable lengths restrictions given in Figs 2.10(a) and (b) are

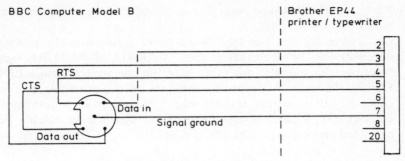

Fig. 3.6 Connecting cable.

observed. However, simply providing compatible waveforms is not enough. This will be discussed more fully in section 3.2.4.

3.2.3 Functional

The functions of the signal circuits are relatively simple:

- RTS is the request to send signal from the computer to the printer.
- CTS is the clear to send signal from the printer to the computer.
- Data out is the connection that sends data from the computer to the printer.
- Data in is the connection that receives data from the printer. This is not always used for one-way communication.

3.2.4 Procedural

The computer and the printer software must be set up for signal compatibility. Compatibility includes:

(1) Transmission codes. The computer will transmit in ASCII code. The printer is capable of either ASCII or a typewriter code. ASCII must of course be used for system compatibility.
(2) Data rate. The standard baud rates for the computer are 75, 150, 300, 1200, 2400, 4800, 9600 and 19 200. (Note: the last rate is not guaranteed.) The standard baud rates for the printer are 75, 110, 300, 600, 1200. I have chosen 1200 baud because it is the fastest common data rate of transfer between the two devices. You should note that a higher baud rate does not necessarily mean faster printing because speed is limited by the mechanical aspects of the print head. Faster data rates will only fill the printer buffer which will in turn signal the computer to stop sending information until the buffer can dispose of its data to the print head.
(3) Bit length. The bit length must be compatible. The BBC computer sends data using one start bit, eight data bits and one stop bit. The printer must be set to accommodate data in the same manner.

(4) Parity bit. The BBC computer does not send a parity bit so the printer must be set for NO parity.

(5) Carriage return and line feed. Some printers automatically move the paper up one line when they receive a CARRIAGE RETURN signal. Since the computer also moves the paper up one line (by using a LINE-FEED), the paper may move up two lines instead of one. In this case, either the BBC computer or the Brother EP44 may be set to prevent this. CARRIAGE RETURN and LINEFEED signals have already been explained previously (see the ASCII code).

3.2.5   Protocol

The protocol between the computer and the printer is relatively simple.

(1) At the commencement of printing, the buffer in the EP44 printer is empty. It is therefore in a position to accept data from the computer for printing and it signals this to the CTS line of the computer with a logic 1.

(2) The computer simply transmits its data for printing whenever it is instructed by the operator to do so. This data will be transferred into the buffer of the EP44 at a rate faster than that which the print head can operate. The print buffer on the EP44 has a maximum capacity of 160 bytes. When this is filled up, the printer signals a logic 0 on the CTS line to the computer.

(3) The computer stops sending data and waits for the printer to empty some of its buffer contents. This state will remain until there are less than 40 bytes in the print buffer. When this happens, the printer signals a logic 1 on its CTS line and the computer resumes sending data until the print buffer is filled once again. This process is repeated until the computer has no more data to print.

In ending this case study, I wish to emphasise that this is one way in which data from the computer can be printed. It is not the *only* way. For example, if data were transferred at 75 bauds, and providing there is enough printing paper in the machine, then the print head can keep up with the rate of data transfer and the print buffer will not be completely filled. The CTS line might not have to be used. Therefore, do not assume that there is only one way of operating an interface, other methods work!

3.3   CASE STUDY 2: RS232, CCITT V24

This case study shows how a computer (Osborne 1) communicates with a high speed printer (Mannesmann Tally model 160). Both units also claim RS232 compatibility but, in this case, the protocol used is distinctly different from the previous case.

This case study will also be discussed using the methods used previously to examine interfaces, i.e. physical, electrical, functional and procedural.

EXTERNAL RS–232 CONNECTOR (labelled 'SERIAL RS232')

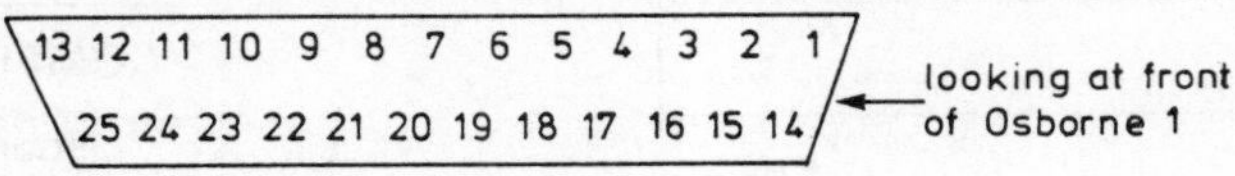

```
\13 12 11 10  9  8  7  6  5  4  3  2  1/
                                            looking at front
 \25 24 23 22 21 20 19 18 17  16 15 14/  ◄─── of Osborne 1
```

1 = ground
2 = transmit data IXDATA
3 = receive data RXDATA
4 = ready to send RTS
5 = clear to send CTS (held + V5)
6 = data set ready DSR (held + V5)
7 = ground
8 = carrier detect CD (held + V5)
9 = NC
10 = NC
11 = NC
12 = NC
13 = NC
14 = NC
15 = NC
16 = NC
17 = NC
18 = NC
19 = NC
20 = data terminal ready DTR
21 = NC
22 = NC
23 = NC
24 = NC
25 = NC

Fig. 3.7 Osborne Model I.

3.3.1 Physical

Both the computer and the printer use the recommended 25 pin RS232 connector but the connected numbers of pins are not the same. The connected pins for the computer and the printer are shown in Figs 3.7 and 3.8 respectively. The four wires necessary for connecting the printer to the computer are also shown in Fig. 3.8.

3.3.2 Electrical

Both signals utilise the RS232C waveforms described in a previous section, but simply providing compatible waveforms is not enough. This will be discussed more fully in section 3.3.4.

3.3.3 Functional

The functions of the signal circuits are relatively simple and have already been described under the RS232 interface section.

RS232C INTERFACE

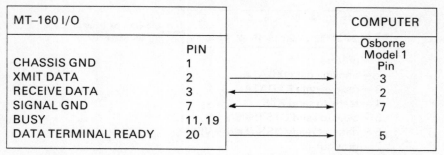

Fig. 3.8 Interface pin assignments – Mannesman Tally Model 160.

3.3.4   Procedural

The computer and the printer software must be set up for signal compatibility. Compatibility includes:

(1) Transmission codes. The computer will transmit in ASCII code. The printer is capable of accepting ASCII code which is used for system compatibility.
(2) Data rate. The standard baud rates for the computer are 300 and 1200. The standard baud rates for the printer are 150, 300, 600, 1200, 2400, 4800 and 9600. I have chosen 1200 baud because it is common between the two systems and because it is the fastest rate of data transfer.
(3) Bit length. The bit length must be compatible. The Osbourne computer is set to send data using one start bit, eight data bits and one stop bit. The printer must be set to accommodate data in the same manner.
(4) Parity bit. The computer does not send a parity bit so the printer must be set for NO parity.
(5) Carriage return and line feed. The remarks made in case study 1 apply here and the printer is set to prevent an extra carriage return when the computer uses LINEFEED.
(6) Protocol. The protocol between the computer and the printer is relatively simple. The sequence of events is shown in Fig. 3.9 and should be read with the text below.
    (i) At the commencement of printing, the buffer in the printer is empty.
    (ii) The printer returns a logic 1 on its DTR (line 20) to indicate to the

Printer	→ DTR (Data Terminal Ready)	Line 20
Computer	→RCV (Sends Data)	Line 3
Printer	→ X_{ON}/X_{OFF} (Replies)	Line 2

Fig. 3.9

computer that it is ready to receive data. The computer sends data for printing on line 3 to the printer. This data will be transferred into the buffer of the printer at a rate faster than that which the print head can operate. The print buffer on the Mannesmann model 160 has a maximum capacity of 2030 bytes. When this is nearly filled up the printer signals a bit character (DC3 in the ASCII code – 13HEX) called the X_{off} signal on line 2 to inform the computer that its buffer is full and that it cannot accept any more data.

(iii) The computer stops sending data and waits for the printer to empty part of its buffer. This state will continue until the buffer is within 132 bytes of being empty. When this happens, the printer signals a character (DC1 in the ASCII code – 11HEX) called the X_{on} signal on line 2 and the computer resumes sending data until the print buffer is filled once again. This process is repeated until the computer has no more data to print.

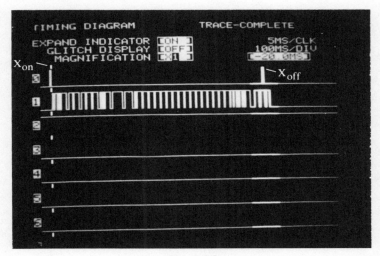

Fig. 3.10

The use of the X_{on} and X_{off} signal is illustrated in Fig. 3.10, which is a photograph of the communication (handshake) signals between the printer and the computer. The first line shows the X_{on}/X_{off} signals from the printer. The second line is the data sent from the computer to the printer. Note that data stops after the X_{off} signal from the printer is sent, and resumes when X_{on} is sent. In order to show the X_{on}/X_{off} signals, I have had to compress the time scale of the picture and this is the reason why you do not see the actual digital bits which make up the X_{on}/X_{off} and the data characters.

3.4 CASE STUDY CONCLUSIONS

The conclusions to be drawn from these two case studies are:

(1) Claims to an interface compatibility for a particular device may not

necessarily mean that the device will communicate with any other device claiming compatibility to the same interface. Most interface standards are not comprehensive enough.

(2) Electrical waveform compatibility is not enough. Even when two identical devices are made to communicate, care must be taken to ensure that they use the same protocol, data rate, transmission codes, timing signals, etc.

(3) Care must be exercised in choosing connecting cables because end connectors may differ. It should also be noted that some pins are strapped together within a cable. For example, pins 4 and 5 are frequently strapped together to give the host device the impression that its RTS signal on pin 4 has been answered by CTS on pin 5. In fact, there are many cables which strap pins 4, 5, 6 and 8 together.

(4) Finally, it is vitally important to understand the functions of the circuits which are to be interfaced so that any problem area may be located.

CHAPTER 4
Local Area Networks

4.0   LOCAL AREA NETWORKS

Local area networks (LANs) are communications networks used between computers and their associated equipment.

4.1   INTRODUCTION

The work on *local area networks* will be presented in the next four chapters. In this chapter I will introduce you to background material on local area networks, their purposes, uses and the techniques used for the transmission of signals. This will allow you to apply this information to most of the existing local area networks in service.

In chapter 5 I will apply your background knowledge to two practical local area networks, called *Ethernet* and *Cheapernet*. In chapter 6 I will introduce you to some *network interconnection* and *modem* techniques which enable local area networks to be joined together to form wide area and global area networks.

In chapter 7 I will introduce you to the architecture of an ideal local area network, called the *Open System Interconnection* model. This is the model envisaged by the International Systems Organisation (ISO), European Computers Manufacturers' Association (ECMA) and CCITT.

4.2   OVERVIEW

4.2.1   Area

A local area network (LAN) is primarily a data transmission system intended to link computers and associated devices within a restricted geographical area. The linking distances are relatively short, with cable lengths rarely exceeding 5 km. The linked computers may include full scale main frame computers, word processors and/or desk top computers. The associated devices could range from computer terminals, video display units (VDUs) to printers.

The key characteristic of a LAN is the fact that the whole of the network is usually confined to one site and that it is completely under the control of one organisation. A typical example of such a system would be that of communications within a large factory site, where several computers in different buildings would be used to communicate with a control centre within the site.

4.2.2 Application

The applications of a local area network are many and varied and could include file transfer and access, word processing, electronic message handling, electronic control, remote data base access and other similar functions.

The exclusive use of a dedicated network such as a LAN to a specific purpose brings many advantages. High data transmission rates can be achieved by utilising the advantages of short distances and the latest electronic circuits. (You have already encountered this in the discussion on the X21 interface.) Thus local area networks are typified by short distances (up to 5 km, although 1 km is more usual), by a high transmission rate (0.1 to 20 Mbps) and by a low error rate.

4.3 DESIGN GOALS OF LANS

Local area networks are designed to fulfil as many as possible of the goals listed below.

4.3.1 High data transmission rates

High data transmission rates are desirable because they permit more information to be transmitted in a given time and hence more efficient traffic handling capacity. Digital transmission rates of 10 Mbps are common; transmission rates of 100 Mbps are expensive but available. However, it should be stressed that the actual data transferred is less than the data transmission rate because some of the data sent is used to establish overheads (control signals, addresses, etc.).

4.3.2 Low error rates

Low error rates are obviously desirable. Bit error rates of 1 part in 10^9 are more easily achievable in LANs, because (1) the transmission distances are relatively short, thus minimising signal attenuation, noise, and interference pickup, and (2) error correction schemes from the simple parity checks to more complex cyclic redundancy checks (CRC) can be carried out. In practice, the undetected error rate is about 1 part in 10^{12}.

4.3.3 Inexpensive transmission media

The cost of the transmission media used should be minimal. The transmission media used in local area networks may consist of one or more combinations of twisted wire pairs, coaxial cables and glass fibre cables. The media chosen will depend on the application. Twisted wire pairs tend to be used where data rates are low and transmission distances are relatively short. Coaxial cables are popular where data rates are high. Fibre cables are used where a higher data rate is required.

4.3.4 Interface connections

Inexpensive and relatively simple means of connecting the data equipment to the transmission medium should be used. The physical connections should be relatively easy to make and the connected devices should not load the operating conditions of the transmission medium unduly.

4.3.5 Interconnection with other networks

The ability to interconnect with other networks is another important attribute which LANs should possess. This may be motivated by economic reasons or simply by the needs of users. Such needs may take the following forms:

(1) A computerised mail system in which messages to and from LAN users may be exchanged via a gateway to another network.
(2) Access to specialised computing resources required on an occasional basis but which is economically unjustified on a local basis.
(3) Communications between LANs.

4.4 DESCRIPTION OF LOCAL AREA NETWORKS

There are many types of local area networks and it will be impossible to describe all of them within the confines of this book. However, most LANs share common features which can be categorised under four main headings. These are:

(1) network topology
(2) signalling methods
(3) network sharing techniques
(4) contention techniques.

I will describe LANs under these categories to familiarise you with the technical terms used by manufacturers to describe their products. This will help you towards understanding the basic principles of a particular LAN. In fact, in the next section, I will be applying the basic knowledge you have acquired towards understanding the basic principles of two LANs called *Ethernet* and *Cheapernet*.

4.5 NETWORK TOPOLOGY

A node on a local area network is defined as the interface point to which data equipment is connected. The topology of a LAN is the *pattern* of the nodes and their interconnection. The four main types of LANs will now be described.

4.5.1 Star network topology

The star topology (Fig. 4.1) is the most common topology used for installations which are designed around a main frame computer. The centre of the

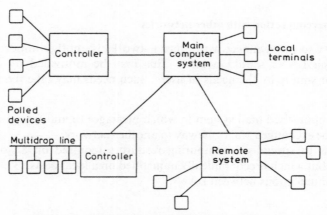

Fig. 4.1 Star Mainframe Computer System.

star (main computer system) can perform processing and/or switching of messages from one incoming line to another. More complex networks can be formed by interconnecting the star networks. The main feature of this kind of topology is that each outlying device is connected to the central system by a line which is for its exclusive use or which is shared by only a small number of other devices. The shared resource in a star network is the central system and not the transmission medium as in the case of a true local area network.

The main advantage of a star network is that new devices are relatively easy to install because each new device just needs to be connected into an existing line, or a new line which is put in between it and the central system.

The main disadvantage of a star network is that additional cabling is necessary between the new device and its connection point. This can be expensive because the installation of cabling between the central system and a device often means accessing the whole route between the two sites in order to put cabling into the ducts. Another requirement is that the communications handling device at the central site also needs to have a suitable node available to communicate with the device being put in. Thus in a star network which is serving twenty-five separate terminals, a communications controller with twenty-five ports is needed with twenty-five separate lines between it and the terminals.

A star computer network generally operates in a polled mode, i.e., a mode in which each outlying device is asked in turn if it has any information to transmit. If it has, the communications controller will either give its full attention to that device until it has no more information to send, or it will allow the device to send part of its information, give another device a chance and then return back to the original device. If the central device acts only as a switch, two devices can be connected together for a time so that they can exchange messages. During this exchange, other pairs of devices can be in conversation without affecting any other dialogues.

The star is an important topology for local area networks. The central device or hub is used primarily as a switch for connecting together the peripheral terminals, workstations, computers, etc. This is similar to the purpose of the normal private on-site telephone networks, where the telephone exchange is the hub and the peripheral devices are telephones. When used in this form, star networks become local area networks with suitably enhanced exchanges at the centre.

4.5.2   Ring network topology

A ring network (Fig. 4.2(a)) consists of a loop with no loop controller. Nodes are connected to this loop. No node is responsible for controlling the network as a whole and each node has equal status.

The aim of a ring network is to provide a cheap and efficient means of connecting together all the devices which have to communicate with each other. The main features are (1) a fair share of communications for all nodes, (2) a simple means of ring control and (3) relatively simple node connections to the loop.

Most existing rings are unidirectional in that information is received on one side of a node and is transmitted from the other side. Bidirectional rings are possible but are more complicated, in terms of the wiring which is required, the control mechanism which must be employed and the higher level protocols needed to ensure that messages are received in order and erroneous ones are detected and retransmitted.

Ring networks usually operate by means of a special message passed from one node to the next. Any node receiving this special message is allowed to transmit a packet of information. All other nodes on the network, upon receiving the information packet, examine the destination address field of the message to determine if it is intended for them. If it is, they read the message into a buffer and in some schemes they mark the original packet as having

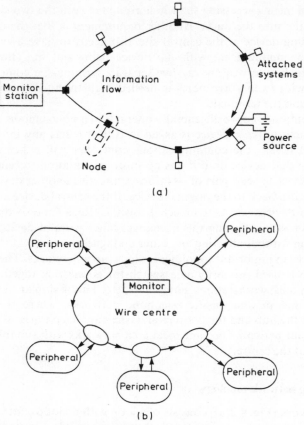

Fig. 4.2 (a) Ring network.
(b) Self healing ring.

been received. Since everyone on the ring can actually receive each packet, it is relatively easy to implement a broadcast message facility.

Rings with raw data rates (overall data rates including overheads) of 10 Mbps are common. Fast rings with raw data rates of 100 Mbps are used in special applications. The actual observed point-to-point information transfer rate depends to a large extent on the methods used to control and access the ring. The mode of transmission is usually direct digital signalling. The transmission medium used in a ring network can be coaxial cable, twisted-pair telephone cables or optical fibre.

Rings are sometimes criticised with respect to their reliability, since the information is circulated through each node, and each node must be able to both listen and to retransmit the incoming transmission to the next node. The hardware which receives and retransmits messages at the ring for each node is called the repeater. It is usually kept separate from the main section of the node. The repeater is powered by current from the ring network and is always switched on to ensure uninterrupted ring operation. The main section of the node is powered locally and can be switched off without affecting the operation of the ring. This enhances ring reliability but increases complexity when fibre optic cables are used because an additional copper cable must be used to supply the power to the repeaters.

Adding new nodes to an existing ring will temporarily affect its operation since the link must be broken to insert a new repeater. Whilst this is done, the rest of the devices will be unable to use the ring. This inconvenience can be alleviated by temporarily duplicating the path.

A special monitor is frequently attached to a ring network to monitor traffic and to remove contaminated packets which circulate without being removed or re-used. This is necessary otherwise contaminated packages will clog the network. Monitors can also be used to pin-point nodes or repeaters which are not functioning correctly, and to gather statistics about the use of the network to assist in planning future developments in the system.

Some rings are said to be 'self healing'. A typical example of this is shown in Fig. 4.2(b). The advantage of such a system is that any non-operational node can be bypassed at the monitor centre to ensure continued communication. Some authorities refer to this arrangement as a star-ring network because it comprises two types of networks.

4.5.3 Loop network topology

A loop network (Fig. 4.3) consists of a loop and a loop controller which has only two cables attached to it: one for outgoing messages and one for incom-

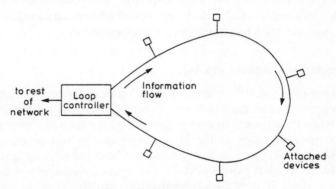

Fig. 4.3 Loop network.

ing messages. All terminals and other devices on the network are connected to this loop and share it to send messages to other devices on the loop. This topology is useful as an optional means of connecting a small number of terminals to a computer, provided that the quantity of information which they each have to send is relatively small.

The manner in which the actual loop is shared amongst the devices connected to it depends largely on the supplier. One way is to poll each device in turn by means of a specially addressed packet. Devices ready to send can then respond in a manner determined by the system protocol. Another way is for the controlling device to send periodically a signal packet around the loop. A signal packet is a group of characters which contain a message. This group of characters will normally include:

(1) Delimiter and control indicators at the beginning of the packet.
(2) One or more destination addresses.
(3) A source address to indicate its origin.
(4) Control indicators to identify the type of packet.
(5) The message itself.
(6) Delimiter and control characters at the end of the signal packet.

However, the signal packet which the controller sends around the loop is empty, i.e. it carries no distinct message other than an invitation for the devices on the loop to use this empty packet to transmit its messages. Any device which has information to send is at liberty to put its data into the packet. With this technique, unless every device sends information infrequently, some control must be devised to prevent one user from hogging the whole network.

The loop is considered to be a local area network because every device on it shares the same transmission medium. Loops generally employ relatively low speed transmission lines with the result that the devices which can be served effectively on it are severely limited both in number and in speed.

Loop topology should not be confused with *ring* topology which was described in the previous section. Loop topology has a controller which controls the use of the network by all the devices which are connected to it. Ring topology does not use a loop controller, it uses a monitor.

4.5.4 Bus/highway network topology

A bus network (Fig. 4.4) consists of a main highway for transporting information between the devices which are connected to it. It is a development of the data bus which is used in computer systems for interconnecting all the various components such as the processor, memory and peripheral controllers. All nodes share the same transmission bus, and each node is given a unique address which the other nodes use to append messages to this unique address. As there is only one transmission path available in the whole network, some scheme for sharing its use as fairly as possible amongst all the devices must be adopted. Such schemes include providing a time slot for each node to send information or a completely random method in which devices send information on a bus master when and if available. In all cases, however, the nodes must be sufficiently intelligent to handle the problems which occur when the bus is already in use or when a collision occurs, i.e. data from one device colliding with data sent simultaneously from another device. The data bus itself is completely passive.

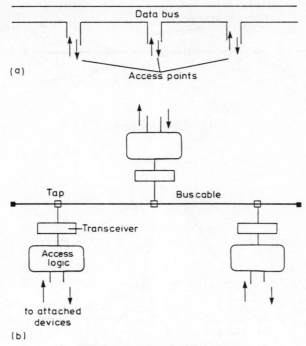

Fig. 4.4 Data bus network.
(a) Conceptual model.
(b) Practical implementation.

Each node must listen all the time to the network to detect information which is sent to it. The nodes must also implement a set of high-level protocols to ensure that the data received is the same as that which was sent, because the high possibility of collision in some systems makes it very likely that information will be corrupted in transit. The method of accessing information on to the bus is the most important single factor in obtaining efficient use of the network.

4.5.5 Other network topologies

A tree network (Fig. 4.5(a)) is also quite commonly used, but it is similar to the bus/highway network described in the previous section. If active devices are at the points where the lines branch (Fig. 4.5(b)) the network can be considered as a set of interconnected stars with each device connected by a dedicated line into the network.

Fully interconnected networks or meshes (Fig. 4.5(c)) are used to provide extreme reliability or to cater for exceptionally heavy traffic. These networks cost considerably more to implement than a typical local area network and are not generally considered local area networks because they do not provide

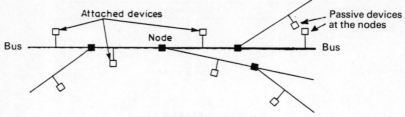

(a) Tree networks.

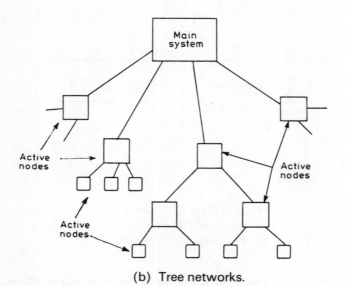

(b) Tree networks.

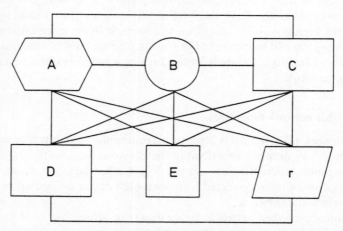

(c) Fully interconnected networks.

Fig. 4.5

a shared data transmission system which is the overriding factor in local area networks.

4.6 SIGNALLING METHODS

The signals used on a local area network must be suitable for the transmission medium. For example, it is pointless sending optical signals through a copper cable – the signals will simply not be propagated. For local area networks, two classes of signalling techniques are generally used: baseband and broadband.

Baseband signalling is popular because it is the simplest method of signalling which can be used in local area networks. The digital signals on a baseband system are transmitted as discrete changes in the signal which correspond to the digital information of the incoming data. Various methods of encoding the signal on to the transmission medium have been tried but the one which seems to have found favour with manufacturers is known as *Manchester* encoding.

Manchester encoding (Fig. 4.6) is one of the simplest to implement and has a feature which makes it very valuable for data communication systems. It

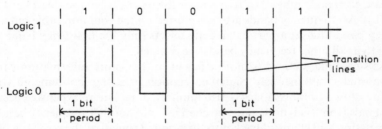

Fig. 4.6 Manchester encoding.

has a built-in clocking scheme which enables every node on the network to remain in synchronisation. In Manchester encoding, transmission time is divided into equal time periods. Each time period is used to represent a single bit, but each time period is itself subdivided into two halves. During the first half of the period the signal transmitted is the complement (opposite) of the bit value sent in that period. In the second half of the period the uncomplemented (true) value is sent. This produces a signal transition at the halfway point of every time period, and enables relatively simple electronic circuitry on every device connected in the network to keep in synchronisation.

4.6.1 Broadband signalling

Broadband signalling is used when more than one communication channel is to be used simultaneously. The principle used in broadband signalling is to

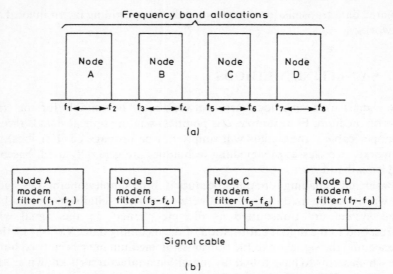

Fig. 4.7 (a) Broadband signalling frequency band allocations.
(b) Broadband signalling node arrangement.

allocate each node a band of frequencies for its exclusive use (see Figs 4.7(a) and (b)). All frequency bands are transmitted on the common cable but a frequency band filter at a particular node selects only the frequency band allocated to it; all other frequency bands are rejected.

The signalling method is more efficient in that more information can be transmitted simultaneously. Signal corruption from the simultaneous transmission of two or more nodes is also minimised. It is more expensive because the signals from each node must be changed into another frequency band for transmission and changed back into the original signals at the receiving node. The system also suffers from the inability of a node to broadcast a message to all other nodes simultaneously. For example, node A can only communicate with nodes B, C and D by transmitting in turn on the frequency bands allocated to nodes B, C and D.

4.6.2   Signalling throughput efficiency

Signalling throughput efficiency is a percentage measurement of the ratio of information transmitted successfully by a network relative to the information offered to it. For example, if the offered data rate in a network is 10 Mbps, and if the transmitted data rate is 9 Mbps without errors, then its signalling throughput efficiency is $9/10 \times 100 = 90\%$. However, care must be exercised in determining how signalling efficiency is quoted. In some networks (described later), it is possible for the same data stream to be transmitted over and over again due to signal corruption, or for control information to be transmitted continuously whilst terminals are unable to access the network. If either of the above conditions are considered to be transmitted data, then the signalling efficiency may not reflect the true transmission rate of data exchanged between terminals.

4.7 NETWORK SHARING TECHNIQUES

Network sharing techniques are used to enable more than one user to use the network without interfering significantly with the other users. A typical example of network sharing is your home telephone, where all members of the family use the same telephone.

Many techniques are used but only a few will be described here.

4.7.1 Time division multiplexing

The time division multiplexing used on local area networks is similar to the bus system used in most processors, in that signal information is conveyed from one device to another according to the needs of the system. One such arrangement is shown in Fig. 4.8. A number of relatively slow terminals

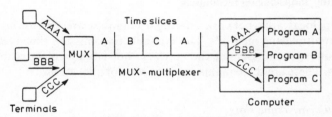

Fig. 4.8 Line-sharing by low-speed devices.

AAA, BBB, CCC, each want to use the common bus line to communicate with the same computer. Communication using the same bus can be achieved by using a multiplexer whose function is to allocate time periods to each terminal so that communication may be carried out without confusion.

Information flows between the terminals and the multiplexer at a rate determined by the terminals. The time slots allocated to each terminal are kept fairly small to enable each device to have frequent use of the shared high speed bus, and to minimise the amount of buffer storage required in the multiplexer itself. The data which passes along the shared circuit is a more or less continuous stream of binary digits or characters. At the receiving end, a multiplexer, synchronised to the sending multiplexer, is used to divide the incoming bit stream back into its original data streams AAA, BBB and CCC.

Time division multiplexing is an important technique for a number of local area networks technologies, especially those based on the ring topology. In rings, each station is normally given the opportunity to use the ring for a fixed period of time. Normally no actual physically separate multiplexer is used, since the mechanisms for accessing the ring are inherently time division multiplexing devices.

4.7.2   Statistical time division multiplexing

Statistical time division multiplexing (STDM) is an extension of time division multiplexing. Experience in using local area networks has shown that some terminals require more use of the network than others. If less time is allocated to the less busy terminals, then more time will be available for the busier terminals, or alternatively, the savings in service time to the less busy terminals can be used to service additional terminals. In STDM, statistics are constantly collected on the network requirements of each node, and the information obtained is used to program a multiplexer which allocates time according to the current needs of the nodes.

This system is very efficient because it does not waste transmission time, but it does increase costs because of the greater complexity of the time division multiplexer. It is not often used in networks which carry small amounts of traffic because the additional costs are not justified.

4.7.3   Ring/loop sharing techniques

Ring/loop local area network sharing techniques are extensions of time division multiplexing methods. The available transmission time is effectively divided amongst the users of the network, but usage is dictated by system protocols. There are three main types of time slot allocation.

(a) Pre-allocated time slots

This is the case where each user is only allowed to transmit information during its pre-allocated time slot. This technique is inefficient because time slots are wasted when users have nothing to transmit. Signalling efficiency improves when the system is busy and when users have steady streams of information to transmit.

(b) Empty time slots

In the empty slot method of using a ring (Fig. 4.9), one or more empty packets are made to circulate around the ring. A terminal wanting to transmit waits until an empty packet arrives at its node. The terminal then inserts its own transmission data, which will include the address of the destination terminal and its own address. The sending terminal also alters the marker (a set of characters) on the empty packet to indicate to all other nodes that the previously empty packet is now in use. The packet is then passed from one terminal node to the next until it reaches its destination address.

The destination node then reads the packet into its internal storage, switches a marker to indicate that the package has been received by the desti-

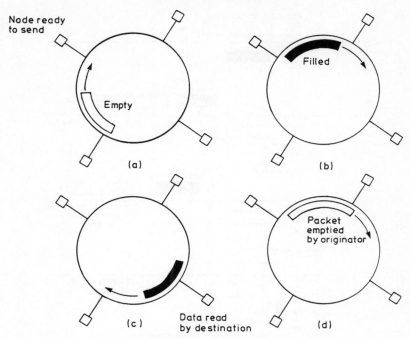

Fig. 4.9 Operation of an empty slot ring.

nation terminal and passes the packet on to the following terminals until it returns back to the sending node.

The sending node then recognises the packet as that which it had originally sent out, switches the used/unused marker to flag the packet as empty and to free the packet for others to use. The same sending terminal is not usually allowed to reuse the same package again otherwise it could claim the package for its exclusive use and prevent other terminals from using it. Hence, the sending terminal has the exclusive use of a particular packet only for the time it takes that packet to circulate once around the ring.

The empty slot technique almost always requires a monitor to spot and re-move defective packets which are not flagged as empty by the originator. It does this by keeping a record of every packet which circulates around the ring. If the same packet is found to be circulating more than once or twice around the ring, the monitor assumes that there is an error in that particular packet, removes it from the ring, and remarks the packet as an empty slot.

The empty slot ring method is also commonly referred to as the Cambridge ring because it is used almost exclusively in a family of local area ring networks developed originally for use in the Cambridge University Com-puter Laboratory system.

(c) *Token passing*

In this system a control token is passed between nodes. Any node which has

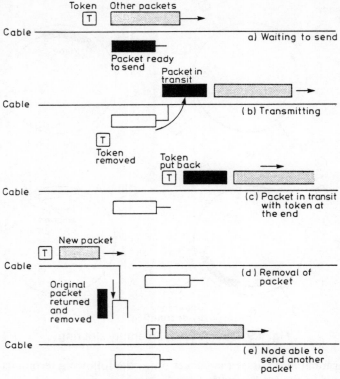

Fig. 4.10 Token passing.

the control token has the exclusive use of the transmission medium and is allowed to transmit. The control token is a packet of information which in itself contains no information other than the right to transmit.

The manner in which a node uses the token is shown diagrammatically in Fig. 4.10. When a node has a packet ready to send, it waits until it is passed a packet containing the control token by another node. It then transmits its packet of information to the network until either the whole message is sent or until the preset time interval allowed for each node to have the token expires. It then transmits the token to the next node which is to have the right to transmit.

The most important requirement of this technique is to ensure that each user of the network is given the token in turn. Token passing is especially useful for ring topologies where it is easy to ensure that the token is passed from one node to the next because data always passes sequentially around the network. Token passing can also be used in bus/highway networks. A typical arrangement of a bus using a token access is shown in Fig. 4.11. In this network, each node can hear every transmission made by every other node and so the token must be explicitly addressed to the next mode which is to have control. The physical location of each node is not in a ring (Fig. 4.11),

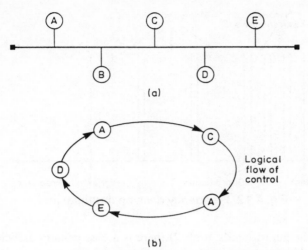

Fig. 4.11 Token passing on a bus.
(a) Physical arrangement.
(b) Logical arrangement (B can only listen).

but the addressing sequence of the token is arranged logically in a ring. Nodes not needing to transmit can be excluded from the logical ring for the passing of the token but they can remain on the bus and be in a position to receive any packets addressed to them.

The logical arrangement of the nodes on a bus can be changed at any time and, in fact, a single node can be included more than once per circulation around the 'logical ring' if it is necessary to give that node higher priority to transmit. Provided the individual nodes are sufficiently intelligent, it is easy to alter the configuration to take account of nodes which fail.

4.7.4 Frequency division multiplexing

A transmission channel has a certain frequency bandwidth (maximum frequency – minimum frequency) which can be transmitted successfully. If the bandwidth is sufficiently wide (Fig. 4.12) it can be subdivided into a number of frequency bands which can each carry one or more communication channels. The available bandwidth can be subdivided many ways. One possible way of dividing the band is shown in Fig. 4.12, but guards bands, bands in which no data is sent, must always be provided between the sub-channels. Guard bands are necessary, otherwise signals in adjacent bands will interfere with each other. Filters must be provided to enable each communication channel to select its particular frequency band.

The advantage of such a system is that more than one channel can be accommodated on a transmission medium. The main disadvantages are (1) the channel bandwidth available for data transmission after the subdivision is always less than the total bandwidth because of the bandwidth loss asso-

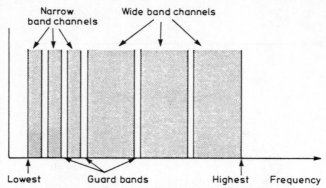

Fig. 4.12 Frequency division multiplexing.

ciated with the guard bands, and (2) there is a cost penalty associated with the additional hardware.

4.7.5 Polling

Polling is not normally considered to be a multiplexing technique although it is a well understood method of sharing one communication circuit among several users which do not need continuous communication. This method is akin to the polling methods used in a computer system between the central processor and its peripherals. An example of such a system is shown in Fig. 4.13. The polling of each device is carried out by means of a unique address which is placed at the head of each polling message.

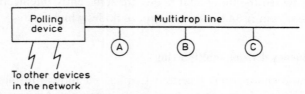

Fig. 4.13 A polled system on one line.

The devices labelled A, B, C ... are connected by the same circuit to the controlling device, which may be a computer or just a terminal controller. If all the devices try to transmit simultaneously, there will be no way of deciding which is to have priority and the signals which appear on the circuit will be incomprehensible. The normal solution to the problem is for the controlling device to ask each of the devices on the network whether it has any data to send and, if so, the controller allows each node in turn to have exclusive use of the circuit for transmitting messages. Various systems of priority can be used to allow busy nodes to transmit information more often than the less busy ones. For example, the busier nodes can be polled more often.

Incoming data from other networks is sent to the controller which adds the address of the destination device to the message before it is transmitted on the circuit. The message is then read by the designated device which recognises its own address.

4.7.6 Bus broadcast sharing techniques

Bus sharing techniques employ a single network. All nodes are connected to this network and all messages broadcast by any node appear on this network and are available to every other node. Chaos results if more than one node broadcasts at a time and methods are devised to ensure that each node has a fair chance of sending its messages. Furthermore, a comprehensive addressing scheme must be used with each message to enable the destination node to recognise the message intended for it.

Methods devised for fair transmission include:

(1) *Time slot allocations*. In this method, the total transmission time is divided into time slots. Each node is permitted to broadcast only within its allotted time slot. The transmission is orderly, but is very inefficient because the time slots allocated to some devices are not used when there is no data to transmit. Efficiency improves when each device has data to transmit. This method is only used in very special circumstances because of its poor efficiency.

(2) *Random signalling*. In this method, messages are broadcast by each device as they are received. Messages which are broadcast simultaneously by two or more nodes are said to collide and become corrupted. Corrupted messages are rebroadcast in the hope that collision will not occur in the next two or more retransmissions. Collision of retransmitted messages can be minimised by allotting different time delays to each node prior to rebroadcasting. Random signalling is useful for very light transmission traffic where the chances of collision are minimal but it becomes extremely inefficient as traffic loads increase.

(3) *Message sense signalling*. In this method, nodes listen on the broadcast network before sending their messages. If there is a message on the network, a node defers sending until the network is free. This system is more efficient because collisions are minimised by the 'listening' before 'speaking' technique but collisions still occur when two or more nodes with messages to send monitor the network, find it traffic free, and transmit. Retransmission with random delays minimises the chances of recollision.

Method (3) is the most efficient of the three methods presented but a set of rules must be devised to ensure that a node does not gain an unfair proportion of the available capacity of the transmission system. This could easily happen when the signal detector of a node is faulty and the node concerned broadcasts continually on the network in the mistaken belief that no other node is transmitting. Other checks must therefore be built into the nodes to

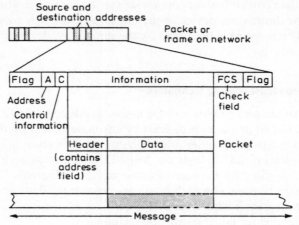

Fig. 4.14 Typical packet format.

prevent such problems. Common checks used are devices which count the number of times a message is repeated and prohibit the particular node from transmitting more than a certain number of times.

4.7.7 Bus packet sharing techniques

This technique is based on ideas similar to those developed for the bus broadcast sharing techniques described in section 4.7.6. This technique compartmentalises complete messages into small packets of information and transmits packets of information rather than a complete message at one time. Each packet of information is provided with headers and trailers to indicate their destination, etc. One typical packet is shown in Fig. 4.14. These packets are similar to the packet frames shown in Fig. 1.26.

The header of a packet includes the addresses of the device which is sending the data and the device to which the information is being sent, information about the packet itself (e.g. whether it contains data or is a control packet), the length of the data field, etc. The trailer usually contains a special field (field check sequence) which is examined by the destination device to see if the package has been damaged in transit and another field which indicates the end of the packet.

Whenever a packet is received by the destination device, the error detection fields are examined and the information contained therein is compared with that calculated by the destination device itself using a previously agreed algorithm. If the two differ, the destination device can transmit a special packet back to the source device telling it that a certain packet has been incorrectly received and request retransmission of the erroneous packet. The source device need only retransmit the erroneous packet and not the whole message. These error detection and correction schemes are similar to those described extensively in sections 1.7 and 1.8.

The length of the packet can be chosen to suit the characteristics of the transmission medium, the devices using the network, or the network itself. Generally the choice is a compromise between the length which is most likely to be transported without error, the time which is needed to place the packet on the network and the amount of usable packet information contained in it in proportion to the rather large overheads imposed by the header and the trailer information fields. Packets generally used for broadcast bus systems are variable in length with a maximum or around 8000–10 000 bits.

Bus packet sharing techniques have very many advantages. These include:

(1) Communicating devices get a chance to input the bus with less delay.
(2) The devices connected to the bus require less buffer storing elements because small packets can be processed (e.g. output to a printer) with relatively less delay, freeing the buffers for more information storage more quickly.
(3) Control information between devices can be exchanged more efficiently because the time delay is less.
(4) Ease of detecting and correcting erroneous information.
(5) Similarity to the format used for standard data transmission, e.g. HDLC signal packages.

Many of the network sharing techniques discussed earlier apply to packet data systems as well but the most commonly used sharing techniques in packet systems are contention sharing techniques.

4.8 CONTENTION SHARING TECHNIQUES

Broadcast contention techniques are especially useful for networks where the terminals connected to it send out information in bursts. It is far more efficient than time division or polling techniques. The success of contention networks depends to a very large extent on the design of algorithms for detecting whether the network is free or in use and stopping transmission if there is a collision between two or more packets broadcasting at the same time. I shall begin by explaining what is meant by the term carrier sense multiple access (CSMA) before describing the methods used to avoid collision detection.

4.8.1 Carrier sense multiple access (CSMA)

Carrier sense multiple access is the procedure where all devices on a network 'listen' (carrier sense) to the transmission medium before accessing it. If there is no transmission then any of the devices (multiple access) is free to transmit a message. (The idea is similar to that of a group of people sitting around a conference table, listening before speaking, to avoid confusion.) However, occasions do inadvertently arise in which several users, sensing no transmission, access the transmission medium simultaneously. (This is similar to

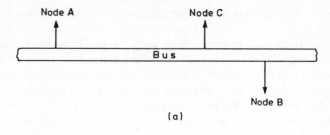

(a)

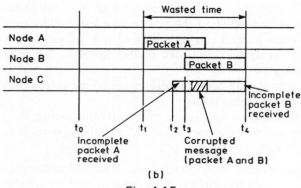

(b)

Fig. 4.15

the committee meeting where several people sensing no speech inadvertently speak together.)

Another problem that commonly arises in local area networks is that shown in Fig. 4.15, where three nodes A, B and C are physically situated at some distance from each other. During the time interval (t_0-t_1) node A senses the transmission medium and, finding it clear, begins to transmit packet A to node C. During the time (t_0-t_3) node B also senses the network and finds it clear. Node B is not aware that at time t_1 node A has already sent a packet because the packet sent by node A has not yet reached the physical position of node B. Node B therefore sends packet B. At t_2 node C has already started to receive packet A but, in the midst of receiving it, packet B arrives and corrupts the message.

In the basic form of CSMA, no notice will be taken of this collision and nodes A and B will continue transmitting until all of packet A and packet B has been transmitted on to the medium. This results in unnecessary wasted time (Fig. 4.15) because all of the packets will have to be retransmitted anyway. Acknowledgement will not be given by the destination nodes. Nodes A and B will therefore have to try to send the packets again some time later.

This basic form of CSMA is said to be *non-persistent unslotted CSMA*; non-persistent because the nodes do not retry immediately the network is quiet and unslotted because nodes are free to transmit at any time.

The wasted time shown in Fig. 4.15 can be minimised if the scheme shown

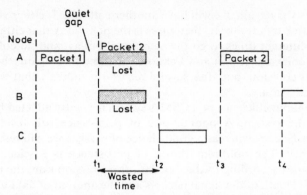

Fig. 4.16 Collision of packets in slotted non-persistent CSMA.

in Fig. 4.16 is adopted. In this scheme, packet transmission is only allowed at discrete time periods, t_0, t_1, t_2, etc. Collisions will still occur but these occur near the commencement of packets, hence there is less wasted time. This type of CSMA operation is called *slotted non-persistent CSMA*.

(a) Persistent CSMA

In persistent CSMA, the nodes try to retransmit a damaged packet fairly quickly after the medium becomes idle. The probability of immediate transmission is denoted by a persistence 'p', where $0 < p \leq 1$. If retransmission is immediate after a collision, then the CSMA is *1 persistent*. This is because the probability of immediate transmission is 1. If the probability of immediate retransmission is 1 out of 10 possible chances, then the persistence is $1/10$ or 0.1, and the CSMA is *0.1 persistent*. Similarly, if the probability of immediate retransmission is p, then the CSMA is *p persistent*.

With 1 persistent CSMA, each node listens until the transmission medium is idle and retransmits immediately. This avoids the transmission medium remaining idle, but it is unsatisfactory in practice because if two nodes retry simultaneously, the signal packets will collide yet again.

(b) Non-persistent CSMA

A non-persistent CSMA system is a system where the probability of immediate retransmission after a signal packet collision is less than 1. The advantage of non-persistent CSMA is that it decreases the probability of recollision but it does this at the expense of allowing the transmission medium to remain idle a little longer.

The principle of non-persistent CSMA can be understood by a simple analogy. Imagine that you and I are both trying to pass through a doorway which is only wide enough for one person. If we both try to get through the doorway simultaneously there will be a collision. If we both back off and simultaneously try again, we will have another collision. If either you or I, or both of us, back off randomly, then there is the possibility that either you or I will choose different times to go through the doorway, and no collision will result. If by coincidence you and I choose the same time again, then we will have another collision, but after several retrys it is unlikely that we will collide again and again.

The throughput efficiency of a CSMA system is greatly affected by the persistence of the system. A poor choice of persistence will result in poor throughput efficiency whereas a good choice of persistence will result in optimum efficiency. The optimum choice of persistence is a science in itself because it varies according to the raw data transmission rate, the number of nodes, the bit length of the signal packets and the amount of data to be transmitted. Some systems automatically alter the persistence to cater for different traffic loads.

4.8.2 Carrier sense multiple access with collision detection (CSMA/CD)

Carrier sense multiple access with collision detection (CSMA/CD) is the most common network sharing method used for bus/highway local area networks. It is a 'listen before and during transmission' system. The advantage of this method over the other previously mentioned CSMA methods is that transmission efficiency is improved because wasted transmission time is considerably reduced.

All nodes 'listen' to the transmission medium. If a collision occurs, transmission is abandoned as soon as possible so that wasted transmission time is minimised. This is shown diagrammatically in Fig. 4.17 where nodes A, B and C monitor the transmission medium. Node A senses the medium, finds it quiet, transmits and monitors its own transmission. It detects a collision shortly after beginning transmission because node B has started transmitting. Node A does not know which node sent the additional message; it only knows that the message on the transmission medium does not agree with its own transmissions. Therefore node A goes on to the collision enforcement

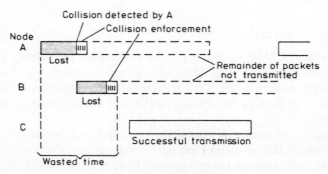

Fig. 4.17 CSMA/CD.

procedure which stops transmission to avoid wasting time and prepares the node for the retransmission of the corrupted signal packet.

Node B is not in violation of any protocol because at the instant prior to transmission it also sensed the medium and found it quiet, because the transmission from node A had not yet reached its physical location. Therefore, node B has the right to send its message. However, after a short time, node B also senses that the message on the line does not agree with its own message, because the transmission from node A has now reached the physical location of node B. (The time for messages to travel from one node to all the other nodes is known as the collision window time.) Node B therefore ceases transmission for the same reasons as node A.

When both nodes A and B have ceased transmission, the transmission medium becomes quiet and all nodes are free to try again. However, each node which detects that its packet has collided with another should not attempt to retransmit immediately, otherwise the same packets will simply recollide. The technique often adopted to avoid this problem is for each node which detects a collision to immediately transmit a burst of noise, to enable all other transmitting nodes to hear the collision, and then wait for an interval of time before attempting to retransmit. If on retrying the medium is busy or another collision occurs, the node concerned backs off for a longer period before retrying. In other words, nodes using the network adapt themselves to the loading of the network. When the network is lightly loaded, the retrying nodes will usually find the medium quiet and so the waiting time between transmission will be at a minimum. When network loading is increased, waiting times will also be increased and the number of collisions will not occur as often as would be the case if the average period before retrying was constant.

In CSMA/CD, specific acknowledgement packets are not generally used because the sending node can sense if a collision has occurred to its message and can deduce whether its message has been sent correctly. This saves time and improves transmission efficiency. If a packet is damaged by some other means, the receiving node will normally be able to detect the error by examining the error check fields in the packet. It is then the responsibility of the destination node to request retransmission by means of a special packet which indicates that the packet was received in error. If the destination node is inoperative, the sending node will not receive any response at all, and a higher level protocol is invoked between the terminals to make the sending terminal determine by means of exchange packets that the destination terminal is in a state to receive information.

Some manufacturers claim that with careful design of the algorithm for retrying and backing off, transmission throughput efficiencies of greater than 95% are possible for all data presented on the network.

4.8.3 Carrier sense multiple access with collision avoidance (CSMA/CA)

Although they do share a number of features, CSMA/CA is not such a widely known technique as CSMA/CD. CSMA/CA is essentially a combination of normal slotted time division multiplexing and CSMA/CD. It operates in the following manner. At the end of each transmission, the time is divided into time slots which are allocated to each of the terminals on the network. The terminal which has the first time slot transmits a packet of information if it has one available. After it has finished, the next terminal in the order of priority is given the next time slot. If any terminal does not have any packets ready to send then that time slot remains unused. If all the nodes are unready to transmit when their appointed time slot is presented, then after they have all been given a chance once, the network reverts to the normal CSMA/CD mode of operation; in other words each terminal contends with the others for the use of the channel. Once the channels have been used again to transmit a packet, the system reverts back to the time slot system.

Normally there is an extra priority given to certain of the nodes so that they are given the first time slots of any sequence. Once theirs have been offered and have not been used, the rest are allocated in rotation. This technique is claimed to be very efficient, especially in networks where some terminals need to use the network more often than others and where the overall loading is fairly high. It should be obvious that the technique can only work well if the nodes attached to the network contain a reasonable amount of intelligence because of the time slot synchronisation and allocation algorithms required, as well as the normal CSMA/CD access methods, which themselves require intelligence.

4.9   CONCLUSIONS

Local area networks (LANs) are a good means of sharing resources such as printers, modems and mass storage devices, while simultaneously providing common information within a company on one site. They offer reliable, fast communications at a relatively low cost.

The *topology* of LANs may be categorised as *star*, *bus* and *ring/loop*. In a *star* network, computers and peripherals are arranged radially around a switching device such as a digital private automatic branch exchange (PABX). The PABX based system is appealing because it points naturally to integrated voice and data communications, with the use of a combined speech and data terminal on one instrument. Because the PABX tends to use existing wiring, data links can be extended to everyone who has a telephone on their desk. It offers a well priced solution to the need for commonality of data and resources. Most such standards are based on the V24 standard with data rates of up to 9.6 kbit/s which is enough for the occasional user but not for regular database searches by several users.

Bus systems are attractive because they do not require a central controller and in some bus networks, such as Ethernet, additional stations can be added at will up to a theoretical maximum of 1024 stations. The traffic on bus systems is non-deterministic, i.e. the delivery of traffic is not guaranteed at the first try but, in real life Ethernet systems, less than 1% of all signal packets are deferred owing to another packet already on the bus. Less than 0.03% of packets collide, so back-off times are invariably short. Bus networks become inoperative if one of the connecting stations produces a short circuit on the connecting bus, but can be easily repaired upon removal of the offending station.

Ring systems link stations in a continuous loop. Data is passed on from station to station on the ring until it gets to the recipient computer. Ring systems allow both voice and data communication, and because the data packets are moving in the same direction there is no need for expensive methods for monitoring and regulating data movement, as with Ethernet networks. Ring systems are more vulnerable than bus systems because if one station on the ring goes wrong, the entire network stops. Repair is not as easy and involves locating, removing and bypassing of the offending station.

Signalling in LANs falls into two basic categories: broadband and baseband. Most networks are *baseband*, which means that at any one moment only one signal can be carried. To allow more than one computer to use the network at once, time division multiplexing (TDM) is generally used. *Broadband* transmission, on the other hand, allows several signals to travel simultaneously by a technique called frequency division multiplexing (FDM). This allows very fast parallel data transmission but it costs more.

The transmission of a signal on a LAN can be achieved in several ways: twisted pair wiring, coaxial cable, fibre optic cables, microwave radio links and infra-red links. Twisted pair wiring comes cheap and cheerful, as it already exists in most offices in the form of the telephone system. It is not, however, the most efficient means of connection. A step up in price and performance is coaxial cable which shields the signal better and allows much higher data transfer rates. Fibre optics, too, offers equally high transmission speeds, excellent shielding, and the ability to carry a far greater number of signals than conventional wiring. Fibre optics is ideally suited to broadband transmission. Microwave (radio) Links and infra-red Links are also available for those who need them. Cost goes up with sophistication.

The optimum choice for a LAN is dependent on the application and finance which is available to the buyer.

CHAPTER 5
Local Area Network Case Studies

5.0 CASE STUDIES

In this chapter I will apply the background knowledge which you have acquired in the previous chapter to case studies of two practical working local area networks called *Ethernet* and *Cheapernet*. These networks were proposed to the European Computer Manufacturers' Association (ECMA) and the Institute of Electrical and Electronic Engineers' 802 Committee in 1983. Ethernet has been accepted under IEEE 802.3 specifications and Cheapernet has been accepted as a subchapter of IEEE 802.3. Some readers may be bothered with the detailed case study of Ethernet. The details are necessary because they reinforce the skills which you have acquired from the previous chapter and because they help you to understand Cheapernet. The details also indicate the level to which you must understand a network in order to implement and manage a local area network.

If you find Ethernet too challenging, then ignore chapter 5 entirely. It will not stop you from enjoying the remainder of the book. You can always return to these case studies at a later date.

5.1 CASE STUDY 3: ETHERNET

5.1.1 Introduction

Ethernet is intended primarily for use in such areas as office automation, distributed data processing, terminal access and other stations requiring economical connection to a local communication medium carrying intermittent (bursty) traffic at high peak data rates.

This system has been chosen because it is used by many companies and because Ethernet is similar in many respects to other local area networks such as Cheapernet, Net/one, Hyperchannel, Nestar, Z-net, etc. There are also a number of relatively inexpensive large scale integrated circuit (LSI) chips on the market for this type of network.

5.1.2 Goals of the Ethernet channel

The following are the goals of the channel:

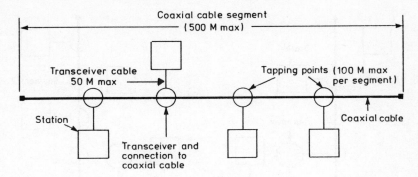

Fig. 5.1 Ethernet topology – minimal configuration.

(1) Provide a means for communication between Ethernet data link entities.
(2) Define physical interfaces so that hardware manufacturers' implementations are compatible.
(3) Provide all clocks, synchronisation and timing required for both the channel and the Ethernet data link.
(4) Provide high bandwidth and low bit errors.
(5) Provide for ease of installation and service.
(6) Provide for high network availability.
(7) Support the Ethernet physical layer to data link layer interface.

5.1.3 Overall views of Ethernet

Ethernet is a local area network which uses a bus/highway type topology. Figures 5.1, 5.2 and 5.3 show possible topologies for small, medium and large scale installations. The system can cater for up to 1024 stations. Nodes (con-

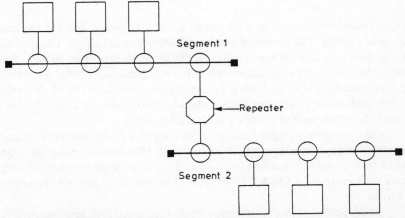

Fig. 5.2 Ethernet topology – a typical medium scale configuration.

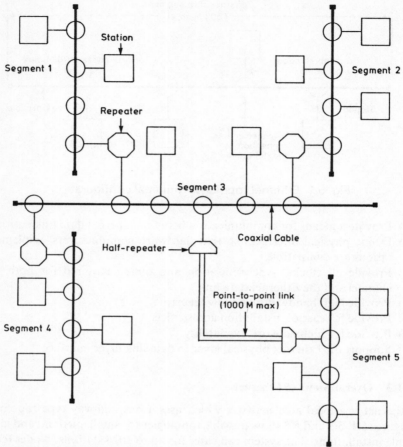

Fig. 5.3 Ethernet topology – a typical large scale configuration.

necting points of stations in the system) share a common bus for the interchange of signals. The common bus is a 50 ohms coaxial cable. The raw data
rate on the cable is 10 Mbps. Traffic on the network is said to be non-deterministic because there is no assurance that a signal packet will be delivered at
the first attempt, but in real life Ethernet systems less than 1% of all packets
are deferred owing to another packet already on the bus. Less than 0.03% of
all packets collide so delay times are invariably short.

Information is exchanged between nodes using signal packets. The signal
packets contain digital data which incorporate Manchester encoding. Signal
packet transmission is carried out using the collision sense multiple access
with collision detect CSMA/CD method. The raw data rate on the cable is
10 Mbps.

The architecture of this system may be divided into three sections or layers
(Fig. 5.4). These are known as the physical layer, the data link layer, and the

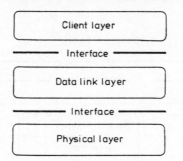

Fig. 5.4 Architectural layering.

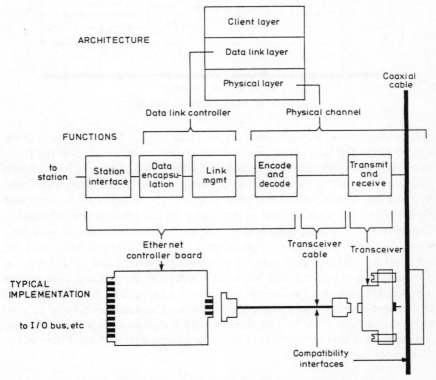

Fig. 5.5 Ethernet architecture and typical implementation.

client layer. The physical layer serves the data link layer which in turn serves the client layer. The physical layer is therefore the lowest layer, whilst the client layer is the highest layer. There is an interface between each layer and the common communication points between the layers are called service access points (SAP).

Each layer performs certain functions (Fig. 5.5) and the manner in which they interlink is also shown in this figure. At this stage, the functions allo-

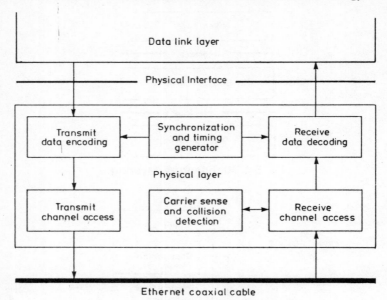

Fig. 5.6 Physical layer functions.

cated to each layer will probably not be clear to you. Do not worry! These will be explained later. However, I do want you to be aware that the functions allocated to the physical layer and the data link layer have been chosen to conform closely to the functions performed by the same layers in the Open Systems Interconnection (OSI) model. The Open Systems Interconnection model is an ideal architectural model set up by the International Standards Organisation. It will be described in chapter 7. Manufacturers of local area networks strive to meet its specifications so that compatibility may be achieved by all local area networks. A detailed description of Ethernet is obviously not possible in this book but I will point out the more important aspects of the system. I will use a 'bottom up' approach in the description of this system in order that you appreciate why certain facilities have to be provided in the higher layers. I shall begin with the physical layer and its main constituents. These are shown in Fig. 5.6 and I will start with the Ethernet co-axial cable.

5.1.4 Physical layer (coaxial cable)

The coaxial cable provides a physical medium for the transfer of signals between nodes. The cable must transfer signals efficiently, that is with minimum distortion, contamination and attenuation. Minimum distortion is important because badly distorted signals result in transmission errors. There are two main causes of distortion in cables: echo distortion and frequency/phase distortion.

Echo distortion may be likened to the distortion you experience when you shout into a canyon and your voice reflects back a short time later to interfere with your oncoming speech. This reflection will not occur if the canyon you are shouting into is either infinitely long or if the end of the canyon is made of such material that all your voice energy incident at the end of the canyon is absorbed and no sound is reflected back. Signal reflection is prevented in the Ethernet cable by a similar technique. The ends of the cable are terminated in matching loads which absorb any incident energy and minimise reflections. However, a signal is allowed to travel along the cable in much the same way that your voice is allowed to travel in the canyon.

A typical example of frequency distortion is the weak and 'tinny' voice which you hear on poor quality telephones. The distortion occurs because the frequency content of the voice has been altered by the telephone system. Frequency distortion alters the waveform (rise and falling edges) shape of digital signals. This causes errors because the signal amplitude might not be at its intended value at the instant when the receiver is sampling the waveform.

Contamination of the wanted signal occurs if unwanted signal is picked up externally on the cable. This is reduced by the use of shielded cable. Attenuation occurs as a signal is propagated along a cable. In a local area network, this is not normally of great importance because the cable lengths involved (< 500 m in Ethernet) are specified.

5.1.5 Interface (coaxial cable to physical layer)

Nodes access the main cable by tapping on to it (refer back to Fig. 5.1). All connections from the nodes to the main cable must be made without disturbing the cable parameters too significantly, otherwise the problems associated with signal reflections and distortion will recur. The characteristic impedance of the main cable is 50 ohms. The impedance of the equipment at the node is more than 1000 times greater than the impedance of the main cable and its upsetting effect on the cable is minimal. Furthermore, nodes are not allowed to be spaced at intervals closer than 2.5 m.

In practice, the actual station is situated some distance away from the main cable bus and interface chips known as transceivers (Fig. 5.5) are used at the nodes to regenerate the signals between the main cable and the terminals. These chips provide the necessary high impedance required by the nodes and also buffer the additional loading caused by the connecting (transceiver) cables between the transceiver and the station.

There are four pairs of cables between the transceiver and the physical layer of the station terminal. These are:

(1) The transmit pair.
(2) The receive pair.
(3) The collision presence pair.
(4) The power pair.

(1) The transmit pair carries encoded data which the data terminal wants to

put on the bus. This signal is generated by the data encoder in the physical layer.

(2) The receiver pair carries encoded data from the transceiver to the data decoder and carrier sense circuitry in the physical layer.

(3) The collision presence pair is used by the transceiver to indicate the presence of multiple transmission attempts on the coaxial cable bus.

(4) The power pair is used for providing power to the transceiver.

5.1.6   Physical layer

The physical layer at the terminal performs six main functions. These are shown in Fig. 5.6 and are:

(*a*) Synchronisation and timing.
(*b*) Transmit data encoding.
(*c*) Transmit channel access.
(*d*) Carrier sense and collision detection.
(*e*) Receive channel access.
(*f*) Receive channel decoding.

(*a*) *Synchronisation and timing*

Data is received from the data link layer as serial words, but these cannot be applied directly to the bus because these signals may not be synchronised exactly to the bit rate of the intended node. A synchronisation signal is therefore generated by the physical layer prior to the data being sent.

(*b*) *Transmit data encoding*

The encoder is used to translate physically separate signals of clock (synchronisation) and data into a single self-sychronisable serial bit stream, suitable for transmission on the coaxial cable by the transceiver. The bit encoding system for Ethernet is Manchester phase encoding. This has already been fully described.

Specifications are laid down as to the permissible delay within the encoder. One such is that the delay between the presentation of valid clock and data to the encoder and the presentation of the encoded signal to the transmit pair should not exceed 100 ns.

(*c*) *Transmit channel access*

The transmit channel access is used to provide a means for serial data to be transmitted to the transceiver prior to transmission on the main coaxial bus. The transmit access channel is also controlled indirectly by the signals from the carrier sense and collision detect channels.

(d) Carrier sense and collision detect

The carrier sense must indicate to the higher data link layer the presence of a carrier, i.e. a transmission attempt on the coaxial bus by any station. This is necessary because the data link layer determines when messages will be transmitted and this should only be done when the coaxial bus is free from other signals, otherwise signal collision and corruption will result. The collision detect is used to inform the higher data link layer that the signal it has sent has been corrupted by simultaneous transmissions from other stations and that the message will have to be retransmitted.

There are rigid specifications for the amplitude and timing of both the carrier sense and collision detect signals.

(e) Receive channel access

The receive channel access is to provide a path for the reception of signals from the transceiver. It will normally amplify and reshape the incoming signal for the receive channel decoder.

(f) Receive channel decoding

The receive channel decoder is used to separate the incoming phase encoded bit stream into a data stream and a clock signal. The decoder must be able to provide the data link layer with usable data and clock signals in spite of the timing distortion allowed by the worst case system configuration. The decoder must provide usable output (clock and data) after more than 16 bit cell times following reception of an encoded signal. The first signals received via the transceiver in a packet are not necessarily valid signals and are usually signals used to synchronise the receiver decoding circuits. The decoder is not expected to provide usable output when there is a collision on the coaxial cable bus.

5.1.7 Interface (physical layer to data link layer)

The interface through which the data link layer uses the facilities of the physical layer consists of three Boolean variables (each of which outputs a logic level – TRUE or FALSE – according to a set of input signals), a function and a pair of procedures. These are:

(1) CarrierSense bit (Boolean).
(2) Transmitting bit (Boolean).
(3) TransmitBit procedure.
(4) CollisionDetect bit (Boolean).
(5) ReceiveBit function.
(6) Wait procedure.

Some of these signals are interrelated in the sense that they work in conjunction with each other. They are also interdependent on conditions existing in the physical and/or data link layer. I have therefore chosen to describe them in this section for the above reasons.

The physical layer monitors the main cable and it sets its CarrierSense detector bit to TRUE if there is a signal on the cable and FALSE if there is no signal on the main cable. The TRUE signal works in conjunction with the ReceiveBit function to inform the data link layer that it must retrieve immediately the incoming bits. When CarrierSense subsequently becomes false, the data link layer can begin processing the received bits as a completed information frame.

The data link layer must also monitor the value of the CarrierSense to defer its own transmission when the channel is busy. This is done in conjunction with the wait procedure. The wait procedure tells the data link layer how many bit times it must wait before attempting to transmit again.

The data link layer also monitors its own transmissions in order to ascertain the proper operation of the Carrier Sense function. This is necessary otherwise the data link layer may misinterpret the signal on the main cable bus as being the signal from another station and refuse to transmit.

The TransmitBit procedure is used if the data link layer wants to transmit. The data link monitors the CarrierSense; if it is FALSE, i.e. no signal on the main cable, the data link layer can proceed to transmit. The data link layer then sets its transmitting flag to TRUE to inform the physical layer that a stream of bits will follow. However, not all of the transmitted data to the cable originates in the data layer. Some of it (like synchronisation) comes from the physical layer so a TransmitBit procedure has to be used to inform the physical layer when to insert its bits.

In addition to the above, the data link layer must also monitor the CollisionDetect signal. This signal is obtained from the physical layer and is TRUE if a collision occurs. This monitoring must be maintained for $2\,\mu s$ after transmission has ended because collision could have happened elsewhere on the main cable after the end of transmission and it could take some time before the signal returns back to the CollisionDetect point.

5.1.8   Data link layer

The data link layer (Fig. 5.7) is rather complicated and, for reasons of explanation, I will divide this into two sublayers. The upper sublayer is called *data encapsulation* and the lower sublayer is called *link management*. Each of these sublayers is further divided into a transmit half and a receive half.

(a) Frame transmission

Frame transmission includes the transmit sections of the data encapsulation and link management sublayers.

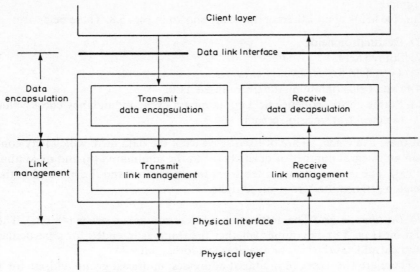

Fig. 5.7 Data link layer functions.

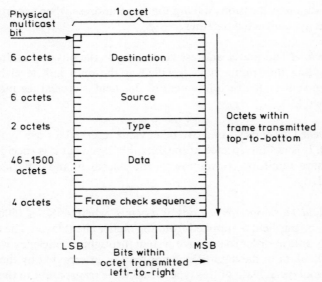

Fig. 5.8 Data link layer frame format.

(b) Data encapsulation sublayer

The data encapsulation sublayer has three main functions: framing, addressing and error detection.

Framing

The five fields of an Ethernet frame are shown in Fig. 5.8. These fields are:

(1) Destination field.
(2) Source field.
(3) Type field for use by higher layers.
(4) Data field containing the transmitted data.
(5) Frame check sequence field containing a cyclic redundancy check value to detect transmission errors.

Of these five fields, all are of fixed size except the data field, which may contain an integral number of octets between the minimum (46) and maximum (1500). The frame is transmitted from top to bottom and the bits within the octet are transmitted from left to right.

(1) Destination field The destination address contains 6 octets (48 bits). The first bit (Fig. 5.8) determines whether the frame is intended for a particular physical address (bit = 0) or a multicast address (bit = 1).

There are two types of multicast addresses: multicast group address for a group of related stations or a broadcast address for all stations. If the latter, then the remaining 47 bits are all 1s.

Six octets for a physical address might be considered excessive but the designers of Ethernet consider this to be necessary in order to prevent two physically different locations having the same address when separate Ethernet systems are connected together.

(2) Source field The source address field contains the physical address of the station sending the frame. It is specified at the data link level because a uniform convention for the placement of this field is crucial for most higher level protocols.

(3) Type field This consists of a two octet value reserved for use by the higher client level. It is not interpreted at the data link layer but it is specified at this level to ensure a uniform convention for the placement and value assignment of this field.

(4) Data field This contains a series of n octets, where $46 \leq n \leq 1500$. The information for this field is supplied from the higher client layer. The data field is made variable in order to improve system throughput efficiency with traffic loading. The data in the data field is not read or interpreted by the physical and data link layers. Data of this type is said to be transparent to the physical and data link layers.

(5) Frame check sequence field (FCS) This contains a 4 octet (32 bit) cyclic redundancy code checksum (CRC) value. This value is computed as a function of the contents of the source, destination, type and data fields (i.e. all fields except the frame check sequence field itself). The cyclic redundancy

code checksum is computed within this sublayer by a rather complicated polynomial. When the receiving station receives its data, it computes this polynomial from the data and compares it with the sent CRC. If the two results do not agree then retransmission will be requested.

The five fields mentioned above complete the frame format of the data encapsulation sublayer which must be presented to the transmit link management sublayer.

(c) Transmit link management sublayer

Transmit management includes carrier deference, interframe spacing, collision detection and enforcement, and collision back off and retransmission. A block diagram of its main functions can be found in Fig. 5.9.

Carrier deference or delay is achieved by monitoring the CarrierSense signal (previously discussed) from the physical layer. When the CarrierSense signal indicates FALSE (a free channel), transmit link management waits for at least 9.6 μs before sending its own pending frame. This delay has two main purposes: it allows all station receivers to recover and provide a minimum inter frame spacing of 9.6 μs. Collision handling, detection and enforcement, back off and retransmission decisions are also made at this level. Notice of collision detection is provided by the CollisionDetect signal from the physical layer. Back off and retransmission have already been discussed under CSMA/CD. The scheduling of retransmissions is usually based on algorithms installed by the system designer in the software.

(d) Frame reception

Frame reception includes the receive sections of the data encapsulation and link management sublayers, and for clarity in understanding these functions I will refer you back to Fig. 5.9 for the main functions which have to be carried out before data can be presented to the client layer.

(e) Receive link management

Receive link management's main function is the filtering out of collision fragments from complete incoming frames. A quick referral back to Fig. 5.8 and a small addition will show that the minimum and maximum number of octets allowed in a frame format are 64 and 1518 respectively. Receive link management checks each frame received. Any frame containing less than 64 octets is presumed to be a fragment resulting from a collision and is discarded. Occasional collisions are a normal part of the link management procedure, and the discarding of such a fragment is not reported as an error to the client layer.

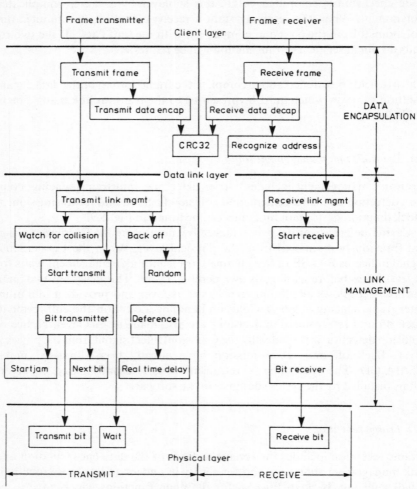

Fig. 5.9 Structure of the data link procedural model.

(f) Receive data decapsulation

Receive data decapsulation functions include frame checking, address recognition, frame check sequence validation and frame disassembly to pass the field of the received frame to the client layer.

Receive data decapsulation checks for maximum frame size and is allowed to truncate frames longer than the allowed 1518 maximum, but it reports this as an implementation error. It also checks the frame for an integral number of octets; non-integral octets immediately signify collision and alignment-Error is reported. Receiver data decapsulation checks its own physical address to verify if the format is intended for itself and for the various forms of multicast addresses discussed earlier.

Frame check sequence validation is also carried out. If the bits calculated from the incoming frame do not generate a cyclic redundancy check value identical to the one received, an error has occurred and it is reported.

Last but not least, the frame is disassembled and the fields are passed to the client layer via the output parameters of the ReceiveFrame operation.

5.1.9 Interface (data link layer to client layer)

The position of this interface in the network architecture is shown in Fig. 5.10. This interface must allow the two primary services, frame transmission

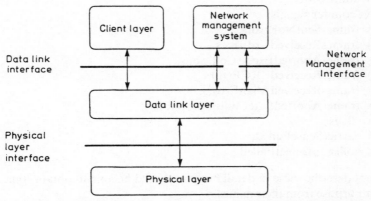

Fig. 5.10 Architecture including network management interface.

and frame reception, between the data link and client layers to be carried out. The interface therefore caters for two functions called TransmitFrame and ReceiveFrame. The client layer is also interested in knowing the status of the two functions, hence TransmitFrame status and ReceiveFrame status are used.

Common TransmitFrame status codes are:

(1) transmitOKNoCollision,
(2) transmitOKOneCollision,
(3) transmitOKMultipleCollision,
(4) CollisionError,
(5) lateCollisionError,
(6) dataLinkOff.

The above are self-explanatory. Common ReceiveFrame status codes are:

(1) receiveOK,
(2) frameCheckError,
(3) alignmentError,
(4) dataLinkOff.

Again these status codes are self-explanatory.

5.1.10   Interface (network management system to data link layer)

This interface is necessary for communication between the network management system and the data link layer. Its position in the network architecture may be found in Fig. 5.10. The signals which must be carried on this interface include:

(1) Four variables:
  (a) dataLinkOn,
  (b) physicalAddress,
  (c) multicastOn,
  (d) addressMode.
(2) Five counter signals:
  (a) framesSentNoErrors,
  (b) framesReceivedNoErrors,
  (c) framesAbortedExcessCollisions,
  (d) framesReceivedCRCErrors,
  (e) framesReceivedAlignErrors,
  (f) framesAbortedLateCollision(optional).
(3) Two flags:
  (a) carrierSenseFailed,
  (b) collisionDetectFailed

I will not describe these in detail but you should be able to obtain some idea of their purpose from their names.

5.1.11   Network management system

The duties of the network management system are:

(1) Initiate, suspend and resume operations.
(2) Read or set addresses.
(3) Observe data link activity.
(4) Check operation of physical channel.

(1) Initiate, suspend and resume operations. Network management can initiate, suspend or resume the operation of the data link interface. Suspension never interrupts a frame transmission or reception that is already in progress; it takes effect immediately after the operation in progress is completed. The operation of the network management interface cannot be suspended.
(2) Read or set addresses. Network management can set the two main addressing modes: promiscuous and normal. The promiscuous mode accepts all frames regardless of destination address. The normal mode accepts only frames with the broadcast address, the station's physical address or, when enabled, multicast address.
(3) Observe data link activity. This facility is used for book keeping purposes

to monitor frames sent, frames aborted, frames received with errors such as align, cyclic redundancy, etc.

(4) Check operation of physical channel. The data link layer maintains two flags indicating, when raised, that a malfunction of the carrier sense or collision detect mechanisms has been observed. Only network management can reset these flags. A network management system monitoring these flags can log the state of the data link in the event of failures.

5.1.12   Ethernet conclusions

The foregoing description of the main features of a typical working local area network should help you to understand similar LANs. Although details may vary, the main requirements of most LANs are similar. Many of the requirements are also similar to the daily problems we face and overcome. For example, in polite conversation, one would always listen prior to speaking to avoid interrupting (CSMA/CD) or one would check the destination address on a letter prior to reading it.

LAN concepts are not generally difficult to understand; they tend to be based on common sense. A practical LAN is really the best compromise of these concepts.

5.2   CASE STUDY 4: CHEAPERNET

Cheapernet is one of the more popular networks. It satisfies the requirement of being a low cost network and yet it still operates at the same data rate as Ethernet. Cheapernet uses the same CSMA/CD protocol, data rate and packet format as Ethernet. It differs mechanically in that it uses low cost cables and connectors and it is much less expensive than Ethernet.

Ethernet (Fig. 5.11(a)) requires an expensive coaxial cable and transceiver cable (four twisted pairs all shielded), connectors (two 15 pin D types) and an expensive transceiver module with a tap that connects to the core and screen of the coaxial cable. Cheapernet uses a T-shaped BNC connector so that low cost type RG-58 coaxial cable can be connected either side to other Cheapernet nodes (Fig. 5.11(b)). The transceiver function, instead of being in a separate box, is transferred to the equipment and directly connected to the BNC connector.

Along with the many advantages of Cheapernet over Ethernet, such as low cost per node, easy installation and maintenance, Cheapernet does have some limitations. Cheapernet segments can be used only up to 200 m, compared to 500 m for Ethernet segments and the maximum number of nodes is 30, compared to 100 for an Ethernet segment. Thus Cheapernet is most logically used for small clusters of stations in an office, such as for personal computers, printers and a small file server.

One simple means of connecting these Cheapernet clusters in a local area is to link them through Ethernet. This is easy because both networks use the

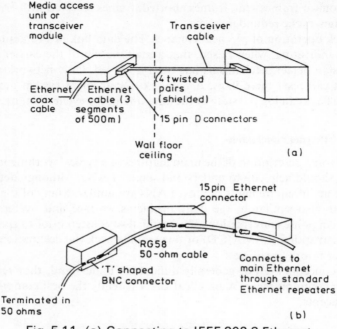

Fig. 5.11 (a) Connecting to IEEE 802.3 Ethernet.
(b) A Cheapernet cluster.

same protocols, packet format and data rate. Each Cheapernet cluster can connect directly through a standard Ethernet signal repeater to the main Ethernet backbone. Standard Ethernet repeaters are used to link Ethernet segments together. In a full Ethernet system a number of segments can be used, such that the total end-to-end distance is less than 2500 m. This applies also for adding Cheapernet clusters to main Ethernet or Cheapernet clusters to each other. There are two advantages in this configuration. The network user has low cost repeaters and the equipment manufacturers that want to provide Ethernet and Cheapernet compatible equipment get commonality of most of the circuitry for both. Repeaters are therefore important for both Ethernet and Cheapernet and a repeater committee has been in existence with IEEE 802.3 since 1983.

Many of the large scale integrated circuits developed for Ethernet will work with Cheapernet and it is not unusual to find repeaters available which can be connected to work with either Cheapernet or Ethernet.

An alternative evolution path will use IBM's token ring as a backbone and Cheapernet clusters connected through bridges to the token ring. One aspect of networking that will become more important is bridging between different networks and gateways to the outside world. This is because different networks with different protocols and topologies will be available. This will be described more fully in the next chapter.

CHAPTER 6
Network Interconnection Techniques

6.0 NETWORK INTERCONNECTION TECHNIQUES

This chapter introduces some basic devices which can be used to connect
local area networks together. The devices also include modems which are
built into many personal computers.

6.1 INTRODUCTION

Local area networks (LANs) have limited geographical coverage. There is
also a limit to the number of terminals (nodes) that can be used on a LAN.
Occasions often arise when a node on one LAN must communicate with a
node on another LAN. This necessitates either joining LAN to LAN or LAN
to WAN (wide area network).

Interconnecting networks can be achieved in a number of ways. The hardware usually consists of a computer (CPU and memory) with an interface to
each of the networks to be connected. The software can be fairly simple or
very complex. The interconnecting device (computer, memory and interface)
must provide additional facilities such as routeing, addressing, flow control
and general network management for the additional information required
for a node on one network to communicate with a node on another network.

6.2 LAN INTERCONNECTION PROBLEMS

Interconnection introduces many problems, mainly because the characteristics associated with a particular LAN may not be compatible with another,
and it may be necessary to change the source node characteristics on one
LAN to provide the characteristics needed for communication with the destination node on the other LAN. Problems vary with the particular networks
involved but the more common problems encountered are:

(1) Transmission rate differences. These occur not only in the networks but
also in the terminal interfaces and terminal software. Transmission rate
difference can usually be alleviated with buffering and storage of data in

the interconnection devices but it is more expensive and time delays inevitably result.

(2) Flow control and congestion control. This is necessary to prevent lost signal packets when buffer overflow occurs. Retransmission of lost packets results in unnecessary traffic delay, congestion and expense.

(3) Routeing. A route has to be found for forwarding the requisite packets on one network to another. Therefore the interconnecting device has to be informed of the routeing or it must be in a position to work out the forwarding route.

(4) Protocols. If possible, the protocols used should be identical throughout the networks. A delay inevitably occurs in the extended transmission and all time-outs (recovery times from errors, etc.) will have to be extended to accommodate the additional time delay. An adaptive protocol will of course be ideal for such a situation.

6.3 DEFINITION OF INTERCONNECTION DEVICES

There are no precise definitions for the three interconnection devices mentioned above, but for the purposes of discussion, I shall assign a meaning to each of them.

6.3.1 Bridges

A bridge is a simple device for interconnecting homogeneous networks and/ or networks using the same protocols. The purpose of the bridge is to make the connected networks behave like a single network by changing the terminal software as little as possible – preferably not at all. Bridges are ideal for interconnecting LANs and are almost transparent to the user. Bridge repeaters are usually used to connect Cheapernet clusters to Ethernet.

6.3.2 Gateways

A gateway is a device for interconnecting heterogeneous (different types) networks. The gateway uses the protocols of each network up to the network layer; the packets passing through the gateway are encapsulated in each network's protocol to reach another gateway or terminal. A gateway is merely a terminal on each network and is given no special status by the network. A gateway nearly always requires an 'internet address' to be mapped into each local network address.

Gateways usually allow terminal-to-terminal protocols to work end-to-end, in the same way that they do across a single network. Each terminal must use two address spaces, one for its local network and one for the network to which it sends.

A typical example for a gateway is the *Darpa* internet system. This uses encapsulation to pass packets containing a common internet protocol between terminals. A global 32 bit address space is used and each gateway maps the 32 bit internet address into a local address for each packet. Binding of the address to the route is carried out for each packet in each gateway. Dynamic adaptive routeing is used. The Darpa internet uses common protocols above the internet layer.

6.3.3 Relays

A relay is used where there are no common protocols or address space that enables use of the other devices. Protocol translation takes place in a relay; thus any device using protocol translation is a relay. Protocol translation usually requires a lot of state information to be maintained about terminal-to-terminal communication. A relay will perform protocol translation at the highest possible level, commonly at the transport or application level.

A relay causes a terminal-to-terminal communication to be on a hop-to-hop basis, which gives each terminal the impression that it is always working with a terminal on its own local network. Measurements and analyses have shown that hop-to-hop systems generally perform more poorly (slower speed) than end-to-end systems.

An important standard that uses relays is the UK Network Independent Transport Service (NITS). This system is capable of working with non-homogeneous networks and with no global address space. The address of a remote terminal is made up of a list of network addresses, each address being that of a relay between networks and the final address is that of the destination terminal. Thus a terminal-to-terminal communication uses a series of network level connections. The problems associated with source routeing of this kind are almost insoluble, and global addressing or naming has been used whenever possible.

6.4 MODEMS

Modems were initially introduced in chapter 2 as network interconnection devices which modified digital signals on computer lines into a form suitable for transmission over telephone lines. Telephone lines, originally designed for voice communications, have limited frequency bandwidth and are therefore only suitable for relatively low speed data transmissions.

Telephone lines are used in three basic forms:

(1) As ordinary telephone lines which are switched at the telephone exchange to provide connection between terminals. These lines are often called 'dial up lines' and are often referred to as lines operating in the Public Switched Telephone Network (PSTN).
(2) Leased lines are telephone lines which are reserved exclusively for the use of an organisation. Modifications are usually made on these lines to allow faster and more reliable means of data communications. There is

also less attenuation and noise on these lines because they are usually connected directly and not switched at the exchange. Leased lines can be two wire or four wire lines.

(3) Four wire leased lines are equivalent to two independent two wire leased lines: Each two wire line is usually dedicated to one direction of transmission to save modem turn around time.

Interest in data communications has grown enormously because of:

(1) Modern businesses and large organisations sending an enormous amount of data between their branch offices which may sometimes be in different countries.
(2) The development of public data banks such as Prestel, which are used by the general public to access information.
(3) The increased use of personal computers for electronic mail and private data.

Some early modems were relatively simple devices. They offered simultaneous two way (full duplex) data transfer at 300 bps. This transmission standard is still in widespread use today for public access networks. More advanced modems are usually microprocessor based and can often be controlled entirely by software to provide additional facilities such as multi-standard operation, automatic call-answering, data rate selection, auto-dialling and diagnosis. Some modems conform to the so-called Hayes protocol which is a 'de facto' standard because it is favoured by many large organisations as these modems allow the use of a wide range of ready made communications software such as automatic selection of frequently used data rates, formats and telephone dialling procedures. Dialling a distant modem and finding that an error has been made in setting up is expensive and frustrating.

Telephone lines are also noisy and some kind of automatic error checking and correction is advantageous when transferring data files. Automatic answering is useful for business use because it allows data to be transferred during cheaper telephone hire periods, e.g. out of office hours. Automatic answering and calling require that both ends of the communications link are set to the same data rate, format and standard and that one end is set to originate the call and the other to answer it. Many modems can be preset to do the foregoing but the really 'intelligent' can set all these parameters by themselves simply by sensing the signals on the lines.

It is now obvious why heavy users of data transmission on the telephone network tend to invest in complex modems in spite of their initial higher costs.

6.5 MODEM STANDARDS

Transmission standards for modems are defined by the Comité Consultatif

CCITT rec.	Data bit/s	Mode	pstn	Circuit type 2-wire	4-wire	Modulation scheme
V.21	300	async	■	■		f.s.k.
V.22	1200	sync/async	■	■		d.p.s.k.
V.22 bis	2400	sync/async	■	■		q.a.m.
V.23	1200	async	◪	◪	■	f.s.k.
V.26	2400	sync			■	d.p.s.k.
V.26 bis	2400	sync	◪	◪		d.p.s.k.
V.27 bis	4800	sync		◪	■	d.p.s.k.
V.27 ter	4800	sync	◪			d.p.s.k.
V.29	9600	sync			■	q.a.m.
V.32	9600	sync/async	■	■		q.a.m.
V.33	14400	sync			■	q.a.m.

key: ◪ half duplex (i.e. each end sending in turn)
■ full duplex (i.e. both ends can send simultaneously)

Fig. 6.1 CCITT modem standards for the public switched telephone network and for private lease-lines.

International Télégraphique et Téléphonique (CCITT). This organisation has produced a series of recommendations, the 'V' series, which deal with nearly all aspects of sending data over telephone lines. Those which concern modems specifically are listed in Fig. 6.1. CCITT recommendation V24 is very similar to RS232, but you should note that many CCITT recommendations are not followed in North America because other standards such as the Bell 103 (300 baud full duplex) and Bell 202 (1200 baud half duplex) have been established.

The recommendations listed in Fig. 6.1 require some explanation because the modulation schemes used with them have not been previously discussed.

6.6 MODEM MODULATION SCHEMES

Modems convert large bandwidth digital signals into a form suitable for transmission over telephone lines in three main ways:

(1) Frequency shift keying (fsk).
(2) Differential phase shift keying (dpsk).
(3) Quadrature amplitude modulation (qam).

6.6.1 Frequency shift keying (fsk)

The principles of frequency shift keying are illustrated in Fig. 6.2. The binary signals to be transmitted have two signalling states, logic 0 and logic 1. In fre-

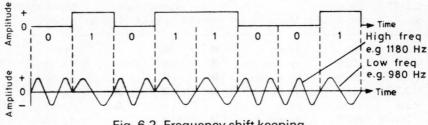

Fig. 6.2 Frequency shift keeping.

quency shift keying, logic 0 is chosen to be a tone, e.g. 1180 Hz, and logic 1 is chosen to be another tone, e.g. 980 Hz.

A digital signal such as that shown in Fig. 6.2(a) is changed by the modem into a succession of tones as shown in Fig. 6.2(b). The advantage of using tones is that less bandwidth is required and it is possible for the same telephone line to be used simultaneously for two way (full duplex) 300 baud transmissions. A typical full duplex 300 baud transmission system would use tones 1180 Hz (logic 0) and 980 Hz (logic 1) for one direction of transmission and tones 1850 Hz (logic 0) and 1650 Hz (logic 1) for the other direction of transmission. Filters are used at each terminal to select the desired tones.

6.6.2 Differential phase shift keying

To explain differential phase shift keying, I will have to jog your knowledge of sinewaves. A voltage or current which varies with time in the manner shown in Fig. 6.3 is called a sinewave; the wave repeats itself after one cycle. The time taken to complete one cycle is called the periodic time. The periodic time can be divided into 360 equal time intervals or 360°. Half a cycle would take 360/2 = 180 time intervals or 180°. Two sinewaves (Fig. 6.4(a)) are said to be in phase when they start at the same time interval position. The sinewaves shown in Fig. 6.4(b) are 90° out of phase because one sinewave starts

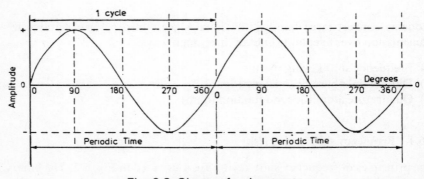

Fig. 6.3 Shape of a sine wave.

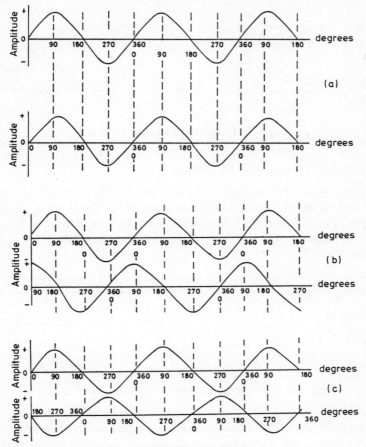

Fig. 6.4 (a) Two sine waves in phase.
          (b) Two sine waves 90° out of phase.
          (c) Two sine waves 180° out of phase.

at the 0° position and the other starts at the 90° position. The difference between them is $90 - 0 = 90°$. The sinewaves shown in Fig. 6.4(c) are 180° out of phase because one sinewave starts at the 0° position while the other starts at the 180° position. The difference in phase between them is $180 - 0 = 180°$. We are now in a position to discuss phase shift keying (psk).

(a) Phase shift keying (psk)

In phase shift keying (Fig. 6.5) the signal is represented by a single tone but the starting point or phase of the signal tone is varied according to whether the digital signal is a logic 0 or logic 1. This is shown clearly in Fig. 6.5 where the tone for each logic period starts at 0° for logic 0 and 180° for logic 1.

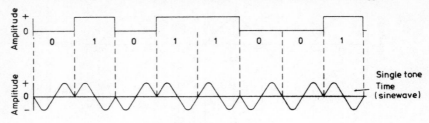

Fig. 6.5 Phase shift keying (P.S.K.).

(b) Differential phase shift keying (dpsk)

Differential phase shift keying (dpsk) uses the same ideas as phase shift keying. However, the phase shift is relative to the end of the phase of the preceding signal. For example, if a logic signal causes the tone to finish at 30°, then a logic 1 signal will cause the tone to start at $30+180=210°$. This is shown clearly in Fig. 6.6.

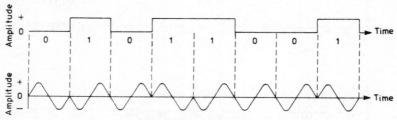

Fig. 6.6 Differential phase shift keying (D.P.S.K.).

Differential phase shift keying is used in preference to phase shift keying on long transmission routes because it minimises synchronisation errors and allows the receiver to extricate the phase shift more accurately. Differential phase shift keying and phase shift keying have the advantages of faster data transmission as well as a lower bit error rate (BER) over frequency shift keying for a given bandwidth but the phase shift keying methods require more complex and expensive modems.

6.6.3   Quadrature amplitude modulation (qam)

Quadrature amplitude modulation combines the advantages of differential phase shift keying and signal amplitude control. Quadrature phase keying uses a single tone for the signal but uses 90° phase changes to indicate changes in logic levels instead of the 180° changes used in phase shift keying. This allows four levels of phase shifts, for example 45°, 135°, 225° and 315°. Four levels of phase changes can be used to represent two logic levels simultaneously. A typical example is shown in Fig. 6.7 where two logic signals 'A' and 'B' are represented in tabular form and with a polar diagram. The important thing to note here is that although the signalling rate remains the same,

Logic level "A"	Logic level "B"	Phase change ° to represent logic level "A" and "B"
0	0	45
0	1	135
1	0	225
1	1	315

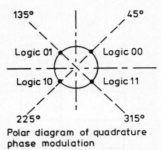

Fig. 6.7 Table showing how phase shift can be used to represent two logic levels simultaneously.

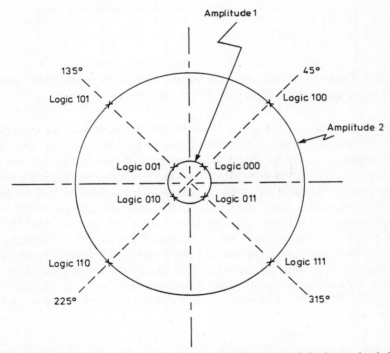

Fig. 6.8 Polar diagram of quadrature amplitude modulation principles.

the data transmission rate has doubled. The penalty that has to be paid for the higher data transmission rate is that the modulator is made more complex and more susceptible to noise pulses because its detector must be more sensitive.

The data transmission rate can be increased further by using two amplitude levels and four phase shifts per level. The polar diagram of such an

Logic level C	Logic level B	Logic level A	Phase change°	
			Amplt 1	Amplt 2
0	0	0	45°	
0	0	1	135°	
0	1	0	225°	
0	1	1	315°	
1	0	0		45°
1	0	1		135°
1	1	0		225°
1	1	1		315°

Fig. 6.9 Table showing how quadrature amplitude modulation can be used to represent three logic signals simultaneously.

arrangement is shown in Fig. 6.8. With this arrangement there are eight possible combinations of signal, therefore it can be used to represent three logic levels simultaneously. A tabular arrangement is shown in Fig. 6.9 and you can see why this method of modulation is called *quadrature amplitude modulation* (qam). The data transmission rate of this modulation is three times that of the signalling rate. The penalty for this data rate increase is even more complex modems and more susceptibility to noise and bit error rates (BER). This process of modulation can be extended but the disadvantages are obvious. However, it does explain why multi-standard modems are desirable. For example, transmission can be started using qam and carried on in this manner until the signal quality deteriorates or until the bit error rate is unacceptable. When this happens then automatic transferral to dpsk and fsk can be used.

6.7 SUMMARY

The points mentioned in the modem discussion should help you to select a modem intelligently. The modem chosen should match the data terminal equipment and the transmission lines. Remember, a transmission system is only as good as its weakest link.

CHAPTER 7
The Open Systems Interconnection Model

7.0 THE OPEN SYSTEMS INTERCONNECTION MODEL

The introduction and the success of the many types of local area networks in the mid 1970s made it apparent that some compatibility would have to be introduced between the networks if their full potentials were to be realised. In 1977 the International Standards Organisation (ISO) initiated work on these requirements to produce a reference model for local area network manufacturers. This model is called the *Open Systems Interconnection Reference Model* of the International Standards Organisation but is commonly referred to as the OSI model. The OSI model is important because it is backed by active participants which include the national standards bodies of the United Kingdom, USA, Canada, Japan, France, The Netherlands and the Federal Republic of Germany as well as the European Computer Manufacturers' Association (ECMA) and the International Telegraph and Telephone Consultative Committee (CCITT).

7.1 INTRODUCTION AND AIMS

The architectural idea of the OSI model is similar in some ways to that of a multi-storey department store where each floor performs certain functions such as delivery, selling, buying, catering and administration. The delivery department is usually at the lowest level because it serves all the floors above it.

The service access points are the stairs, escalators, elevators and lifts which connect each floor or level. The services provided by each floor are defined and you can be sure that if you go to the catering floor you will get a meal. The internal management of each floor is left to the floor manager in much the same way that the method of preparing food on the catering floor is left to the chef. The flexibility in the system comes about because it is relatively easy to replace one set of caterers by another set of caterers and still be in a position to provide meals.

The aim of the OSI model is to remove any technical impediment from communication between systems, even though they may be of quite different

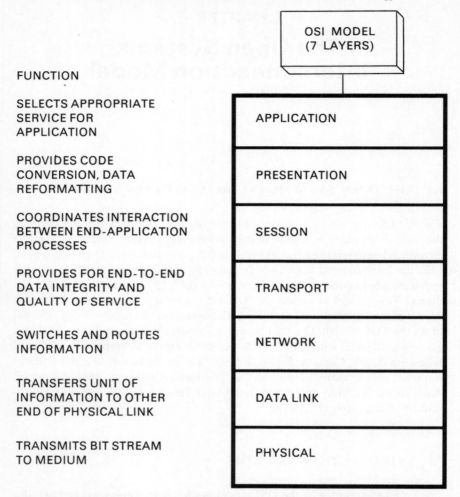

FUNCTION	OSI MODEL (7 LAYERS)
SELECTS APPROPRIATE SERVICE FOR APPLICATION	APPLICATION
PROVIDES CODE CONVERSION, DATA REFORMATTING	PRESENTATION
COORDINATES INTERACTION BETWEEN END-APPLICATION PROCESSES	SESSION
PROVIDES FOR END-TO-END DATA INTEGRITY AND QUALITY OF SERVICE	TRANSPORT
SWITCHES AND ROUTES INFORMATION	NETWORK
TRANSFERS UNIT OF INFORMATION TO OTHER END OF PHYSICAL LINK	DATA LINK
TRANSMITS BIT STREAM TO MEDIUM	PHYSICAL

Fig. 7.1 Functional layering. ISO has solidified a seven-layer structure for OSI. Each layer is composed of functionally separate units that provide specialised services.

origins. OSI is not concerned with the description of the internal operation of any single system; it is concerned only with the exchange of information at the points of interconnection between systems.

7.2   OVERALL VIEW OF THE OSI MODEL

The architecture of the open systems interconnection model (Fig. 7.1) is based on that of structured layers. A structured layer construction is chosen because it provides a comprehensible structure and allows subdivision into individual layers of manageable size, where each layer can be subjected to independent development and maintenance.

The OSI model uses a seven layer structure. The layers are known as:

(1) Application layer.
(2) Presentation layer.
(3) Session layer.
(4) Transport layer.
(5) Network layer.
(6) Data link layer.
(7) Physical layer.

Each layer is chosen to perform one or more functions and to minimise the interface connections between the layers. The hierarchy is such that each layer serves the layers above it. For example, the lowest layer (physical layer) serves the levels above it and the data link layer serves the layers above it and so on.

The upper three layers (application, presentation and session) are generally layered for *processing oriented* functions. Processing oriented functions are concerned with the ability of two similar OSI models to understand each other and to exchange information. The rules required to achieve this are referred to as *high-level* protocols.

The four lower layers (transport, network, data link and physical) are generally layered for *communications oriented* functions. Communications oriented functions are concerned with the use of the physical data transmission network and the rules associated with its use are referred to as *low-level* protocols. Communications between two OSI end system users follow the structured message flow shown in Fig. 7.2. A message generated at the source end (system I) enters the OSI environment through a window of the applications layer. After being processed by each of the seven layers, a formatted message traverses the transmission medium. The process is then repeated in reverse at the destination end (system II). The users are not aware of the processing between layers. To them, it would appear as if they were communicating directly.

7.3 DESCRIPTION OF THE OSI MODEL

The main functions of each layer of the OSI model are described in the following sections.

7.3.1 Application layer

The application layer is the highest layer in the OSI model. It serves the user directly and provides the window through which communication moves in and out of the system. Many different types of application are relevant to OSI. These range from terminal to computer transaction processing to inter-

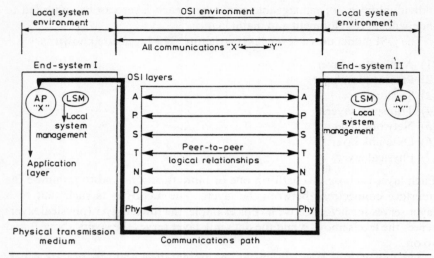

Fig. 7.2 Structured message flow. A message generated in one local system enters the OSI environment through a window of the applications layer. After being processed by each of the seven layers, a formatted message verses the transmission medium. The process is repeated in reverse at the destination local system.

connected real time process control programs. Some of the protocols associated with this layer will be concerned with particular types of application, others will be for general application support.

7.3.2   Presentation layer

The presentation layer performs the two way function of taking information from applications and converting it into a form suitable for common understanding (i.e. not machine dependent) and also presenting the data exchanged between systems to the application layers in a form which they can understand. The layer provides services which can give independence of character representation, command format and, most importantly, independence of machine characteristics.

7.3.3   Session layer

The session layer establishes logical communication paths between applications wishing to exchange data. These two applications form a liaison for this purpose, called a session. The session layer maintains this liaison and ensures that data reaching a system is routed to the correct application. It also ensures that the information exchanged is correctly synchronised and delimited so that, for example, two applications do not try to transmit to each other simultaneously unless full duplex working is allowed.

7.3.4 Transport layer

The transport layer provides, in association with the layers below it, a universal transport service which is independent of the physical medium in use. Users of the transport service request a particular class and quality of service and the transport layer is responsible for optimising the available resources to provide this service. The quality is concerned with data transfer, residual errors and associated features, whilst the classes cover the various different types of traffic which diverse applications require (e.g. batch and transaction processing).

7.3.5 Network layer

The network layer is required to provide the means to exchange data between systems using the network. In particular it performs the routeing and switching operation associated with establishing and operating a logical connection between systems. The network layer also performs the very valuable gateway function of linking two separate networks when these are being used to connect two end systems.

7.3.6 Data link layer

The data link layer provides the functional and procedural means to activate, maintain and deactivate data links between network layers. It ensures reliable data transfer across a physical link by providing the frame synchronisation, error detection and possibly error recovery for the transmitted data. The services performed by the data link include:

(1) Data link establishment, i.e. it creates a logical association between the ends of the physical link and provides for the transfer of data units between network entities.
(2) Data unit transfer identifies the beginning and end of a transmitted frame.
(3) Error notification, like other similar higher-layer services, indicates unrecovered errors that occur between the ends of the transmission medium to the above network for further recovery action.
(4) Flow control regulates the flow of the data units across the link.
(5) Downward multiplexing provides multiple link capabilities for a single network entity, thereby facilitating a higher reliability and graceful degradation as transmission link fails.

7.3.7 Physical layer

The physical layer provides the electrical, mechanical and procedural characteristics to activate, maintain and deactivate a physical connection. Its services include:

(1) Physical connection.
(2) Data unit transmission. This service provides, however, only for the bit transmission of data. A data unit at this layer is a single bit.
(3) Fault condition notification.

7.4 FUNCTIONS, PRIMITIVES AND PROTOCOLS

Each layer in the OSI model has been organised to
(1) perform certain functions,
(2) provide service to the layer above it (if it exists) and
(3) use the services provided to it by the lower layer (if it exists).

Such a layer (denoted generally as layer N) is shown in Fig. 7.3. The N layer (service provider) then provides service to the $N+1$ layer (service user) above it and receives service from the $N-1$ layer below it.

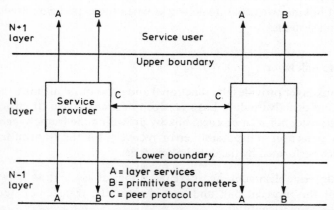

Fig. 7.3 Primitives and protocols. Services are provided by subjoining layers to higher layers. This is done with primitives and parameters, exchanged between layers, that indicate certain conditions and activate the layers' functional entities. Additionally, a peer protocol handles interaction between units of the same layer.

The concept of service between layers implies three essential points: functions, primitives and protocols.

7.4.1 Functions

A function is a logical entity that accepts one or more inputs (arguments) and produces a single output (value) determined by the nature of the function. Functions grouped in a collective unit are defined as an N layer having an $N+1$ layer as an upper boundary and an $N-1$ layer as the lower boundary.

7.4.2 Primitives

Primitives are interactions between adjacent layers in the form of request and indications (or responses). Primitives can also have associated parameters which convey additional information between layers.

Primitives are further subdivided into four main types. These are:

(1) Request – a primitive issued by a service user to invoke some procedure.
(2) Indication – a primitive issued by a service provider either to invoke some procedure or to indicate that a procedure has been invoked by the service user at the peer service access point.
(3) Response – a primitive issued by a service user to complete, at a particular service access point, some procedure previously invoked by an indication at that service access point.
(4) Confirm – a primitive issued by a service provider to complete, at a particular service access point, some procedure previously invoked by a request at that service access point. Note the above subprimitives correspond to the major stages in an exchange between service users. However, it is not essential that all four types of primitives be used in a communication.

7.4.3 Peer protocols

Peer protocols are sets of rules which provide the necessary procedures for the functional units within a specific layer to interact with each other and exchange information. Each layer uses a different set of protocols to communicate with the layers adjacent to it. However, the same purpose protocol used by a particular layer in the source OSI model is also used by its equivalent peer layer in the destination OSI model. For example, if a CCITT type X.25 interface protocol is used by the network layer in the source OSI model then an X.25 interface protocol will also be used by the network layer in the destination OSI model.

7.5 COMMUNICATIONS BETWEEN OSI SYSTEMS

Communications between OSI systems can be followed by referring to an actual case description. For this particular example I will use the particular case of a basic point-to-point X.25 packet switching OSI network.

Referring to Fig. 7.2, I shall assume that an application processor 'X' at the source end (system I) requests the local system management (LSM) to establish a connection with the application processor 'Y' in the destination end (system II). In conjunction with this request, AP 'X' also provides the parameters required for the communication. These may include the address (or identification) of the destination AP 'Y', the maximum acceptable error

130   *Introduction to Data Communications and LAN Technology*

rate, the desired throughput and any other requirements. The LSM determines the availability of the open communications environment (OCE) and initialises the layer entities with the appropriate request primitives.

The connection to end system is the constructed line starting from the physical layer. The physical circuit is first activated and then the data link layer is notified by an indication primitive. The data link entity then establishes its logical relationship, using the data link protocol, with the data link entity in the network. This enables the network protocol to establish a connection through the packet switching nodes in the network.

On completion of the network connection to the destination, the transport layer is notified with a *connection established* primitive. The transport protocol then establishes an end-to-end transport connection with the corresponding transport entity at the other end. In the same way, each remaining layer establishes itself, using the layer peer protocol, with its peer entity at the distant end of the connection. The peer entity handshakings for each layer need not be done sequentially. They may be done concurrently and transmitted as one composite block of information during the network call establishment.

Once the OCE is fully established, full communication of data can proceed. Some data from the source AP may have already been passed to the destination AP during the establishment phase but, in this example, data exchange will commence only after the connection is fully established.

Some idea of how a signal packet frame is constructed can be obtained by referring to Fig. 7.4. The unit of data (AP data) from AP 'X' is passed to the application layer where an application header (AH) for the peer protocol is attached. The AH contains the control information for the peer application entity at the destination. The combination of the AH and the AP becomes the data unit that is then passed to the presentation layer.

Likewise, a presentation header (PH) is added to convey information to the peer presentation entity. A functional unit in the presentation layer performs any code or format conversions needed to facilitate understanding or further translation by the application process at the destination end. Sequentially, the data unit, with the concatenated header, is passed to the next lower layer for further processing. At any given layer, the data unit is the AP data with headers of each above layer attached. Each header conveys to the peer entity the necessary control information to facilitate the defined function of every layer.

Continuing at the network layer, an X.25 data packet header will be added; then at the data link layer, the opening flag (F), address (A) and control (C) information are appended to the front of the data unit (referred to as the 'I' field in LAP B specification of X.25) and the frame check sequence (FCS) and closing flag (F) are attached at the end. Next, at the physical layer, the total package appears as a single frame which is passed on bit by bit to the transmission media.

At the destination end the frame enters the physical layer, where it is passed directly to the data link layer. The data unit is then passed to the next higher layer, the first layer's header is stripped off and processed by the

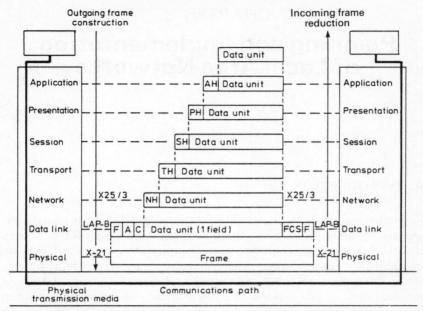

Fig. 7.4 Frame construction. The application–process data unit is appended with a control header (containing information defined in the peer protocol) by each of the seven functional layers. The original data combined with the header of a specific layer, is viewed by the subjoining layer as an integral data unit.

layer's functional unit. Finally, at the application layer, the application header is removed, acted on and the data from AP 'X' is passed on to AP 'Y'.

The APs may continue to pass data back and forth in this manner during the connection. When they are finished a request is made, typically by the initiating AP, to terminate the connection and to free the resources for subsequent communications.

The scenario I have just given you is only one example of a possible OSI communication using the reference model. Other scenarios can be drawn and many can become very complex. However, the OSI model provides a very flexible method of interconnection between different types of networks and it remains the goal of the ISO that the reference model accommodates as many application processes as possible.

CHAPTER 8
Planning and Implementation of Local Area Networks

8.0 INTRODUCTION

The confusing array of local area network technology and the multitudinous suppliers certainly threaten to ensnare the unwary. Successful local area network (LAN) implementations have always addressed defined user requirements, particularly when these requirements are viewed in a strategic context. Often the LAN is but one potential solution to a communication or interface problem. For example, if a communications system only requires three or four terminals with infrequent data transmissions, alternatives such as the switched telephone system with 'intelligent' modems should be considered before the more expensive choices such as LANs, conventional wiring, data process networks, electronic telephone exchange (stored program PABX) and converter boxes.

In view of the above, the planning and implementation of a LAN is not an easy task. Modern business organisations require a combination of many telecommunications technologies for survival. Branch offices must communicate with other branch offices or factories and with the Head Office. Many of the branches may not even be in the same country. Most organisations will already have telephone, telex and facsimile services and many will have several mainframe and personal computers used for information services, control processes and general data information storage and retrieval systems. Direct access to these data banks may not always be possible or certain parts of the information may be classified. Local area networks could prove to be an ideal means of disseminating this information.

8.1 PLANNING

The planning of local area networks should only be undertaken in the context of an overall communications strategic plan for an organisation. Figure 8.1 illustrates some of the major activities which should be carried out in the formulation of a communications strategy. The implementation of such a plan will generally take some time and the plan should be viewed in the context of present and future equipment over a period of several years. The life expectancy of most communications systems is about ten years. Some parts of the equipment, e.g. cabling, have relatively long lives while others do not and it is not unusual for the details of some parts of the plan to be more comprehensive than others. It is vitally important that the plan identifies the appropriate connection points and that the interworking standards are carefully defined at the network interfaces. This strategy is vital if the user is to acquire equipment and services over a prolonged period and remain assured that the network will retain flexibility to meet most present and future needs.

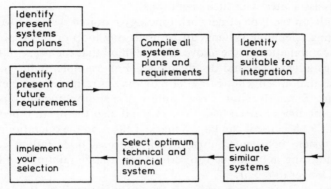

Fig. 8.1 Proposed communications plan.

Most organisations have planned and documented the technical characteristics of their information processes over several years. The plan will probably require reviewing and redefining when local area networks are contemplated. A structural plan should be developed for each local area network and a framework should be defined to enable separate networks to work harmoniously and to blend into a homogeneous network.

8.2 LOCAL AREA NETWORK REQUIREMENTS

The following points should be considered in assessing the requirements of a local area network:

(1) Draw up a functional plan for all the communication requirements for the company. These include telephone services, telex, facsimile and general computer requirements such as data base access and storage, electronic mail and other shared devices such as printers, displays, etc. Can any of these requirements be combined and/or incorporated into the present/future systems?

(2) Translate the functional requirements into technical requirements. For example, if telex is required at various work stations then telex printers and signal cables to the required sites would be some of the requirements.

(3) Access the new requirements. For example, if a mainframe computer is to be connected to various workstations spread throughout a factory site, locate the actual position of the work sites. Work out the requirement of each station, its data handling rates to determine the *type of cabling* – slow speed twisted pairs or high speed coaxial cable – and *length of cabling*, not through the shortest geographical routes but through hospitable routes which will allow minimum interference. For instance, passing cabling through hostile environments such as an electrowelding shop is not advisable because of the electromagnetic fields associated with such operations.

(4) Decide on the type of network topology required – star network if the existing telephone system can be used, ring/loop or bus topologies or any combination of the above. Bear in mind that each type of topology brings advantages and disadvantages. For example, failure of station nodes in non-selfhealing ring/loop topologies results in complete system failure. Similarly, short circuit failure of a station node in bus systems also produces breakdown. Bear in mind also the mean time to repair (MTTR) because it can have a marked effect on the operational time of the system between failures. For instance, a node failure on a self-healing ring may not be too serious but a node failure on a loop will take longer to repair.

(5) Assess also your own traffic requirements as well as the load traffic capabilities of the link. For example, the traffic on Ethernet is non-deterministic and severe overloading of the system will result in longer than necessary delay in the delivery of traffic, whilst ring/loop topologies work much better under heavy traffic conditions.

(6) Decide on the signalling system to be used. Broadband signalling carries much more traffic but requires more expensive equipment. Baseband signalling is relatively less expensive as there are now many large scale integrated circuit chips sourced by many manufacturers. In fact, some LSI chips can be configured to work with either IEEE802.3/Ethernet or Cheapernet and IBM PC token ring.

(7) Define the interface requirements between the elements of the communications plan. Try to use the CCITT interfaces as equipment for these are sourced by more manufacturers.

(8) Revise your plans using different topologies and signalling systems. Is the topology which you have chosen sufficient for present and future needs?

(9) When you have decided on your solution, prepare a tender for your suppliers and be prepared to discuss with them your requirements. State your own or ask the suppliers for their *mean time between failure* (MTBF) and *mean time to repair* (MTTR) rates. When you receive their tender, compare their tenders with your own calculations. Have you missed out any pertinent facts? Have they? If so discuss your apprehensions with them.

(10) Select your supplier carefully. Do not be guided by price alone. Can the

supplier deliver on time? What are the back-up facilities? Is the system chosen also sourced by other suppliers?

8.3   INSTALLATION AND COMMISSIONING

Few suppliers install the local area networks they provide. Some vendors recommend installation contractors, others leave the customer to the mercies of the local cable installation contractor.

Local area networks must be installed with care, and must be carefully and fully commissioned (checked out) before acceptance. The tasks involved include:

(1) Liaison and negotiation with bodies such as architects, main building contractors, electrical consultants, etc., on building facilities and services.
(2) Liaison and negotiation with suitable LAN installation contractors on topics such as methods of installation, testing of cables, protection of cables, hostile environment, etc.
(3) Liaison and negotiation with suitable LAN suppliers and installation contractors on management concerns such as maintenance contracts, provision of test equipment, provision of spares and repair services.
(4) Co-ordination of the various contractors and suppliers to ensure the smooth introduction of the chosen system into service.
(5) Review the effectiveness of the installed system and advise on any modifications which may be required.

8.4   CONCLUSIONS

From the above, you will no doubt realise that the selection of LANs is not easy. Even if the above requirements are carried out faithfully, there is every possibility that certain factors may be overlooked. You have seen this quite clearly when Ethernet was described in more detail. Initially it appeared to be relatively simple but a study of it did reveal the problems which would be encountered.

If one or more problems arise, the best procedure is not to panic and to solve the problems systematically, otherwise the installed LAN may become a liability rather than an asset.

CHAPTER 9
Finale

Congratulations! You have now completed this unit whose main purpose has been to provide you with an introduction to computer and data communications and networks.

The information you have acquired in this book will guide you towards finding additional details of other interfaces or networks. In order to aid you in that direction, I have provided you with:

List of abbreviations	appendix A
Glossary of technical Terms	appendix B
List of CCITT V recommendations	appendix C
List of CCITT X recommendations	appendix D
List of reference books	appendix E
List of technical papers	appendix F

The list of abbreviations is useful because it allows you to refer back at a later date, should you forget the meaning of an abbreviation.

The glossary of technical terms is only intended to be used to jog your memory. The definitions given are not intended to be used in a court of law.

The CCITT V and X recommendations can be used to guide you to an original CCITT document.

The list of books provides useful information for background reading. *Computer Network Architectures* is not a particularly easy book to read but it does provide a comprehensive bibliography of articles.

The technical papers and magazine articles will inevitably age but once you get to know the name of the journals, updating becomes easier.

Finally, let me wish you every success in your future work.

List of Abbreviations
used in Communications

A   Ampere
ACK   Acknowledgement
ACU   Automatic call unit
A/D   Analogue to digital
ADCCP   Advanced data communication control procedure
AM   Amplitude modulation
ANSI   American National Standards Institute
ARM   Asynchronous response mode
ARPA   Advanced Research Projects Agency
ARQ   Automatic send/receive
ASCII   American standard code for information interchange
ATDM   Asynchronous time division multiplexing

BCC   Block control character or block character check
BER   Bit error rate
BSC   Binary synchronous communication
BSI   British Standards Institution
BT   British Telecom

CCITT   Comité Consultatif International Telegraphique et Telephonique
CEPT   Conference Europene des Administration des Postes et des Tele-
communications
C/N   Carrier to noise ratio
COMSAT   Communications satellite
CRC   Cyclic redundancy check
CSMA   Carrier sense multiple access
CSMA/CA   Carrier sense multiple access with collision avoidance
CSMA/CD   Carrier sense multiple access with collision detection
CTS   Clear to send

D/A   Digital to analogue
DC   Device control
DCA   Defence Communications Agency
DCD   Data carrier detect

DCE   Data circuit terminating equipment
DDCMP   Digital data communication message protocol
DEUNA   Digital Ethernet to Unibus network adapter
DIANE   Direct access information network – Europe
DLE   Data link escape
DNA   Digital network architecture
DPSK   Differential phase shift keying
DSE   Data switching exchange
DTE   Data terminal equipment

EBCDIC   Extended binary coded decimal interchange code
ECMA   European Computer Manufacturers' Association
EIA   Electronics Industries Association
EIN   European Informatics Network
ENQ   Enquiry
EOB   End of block
EOM   End of message
EOT   End of transmission
ESC   Escape
ETB   End of transmission
ETX   End of text
Euronet   European online information network

F   Farad – unit of electrical capacitance
FD(X)   Full duplex
FDM   Frequency division multiplex
FDMA   Frequency division multiple access
FM   Frequency modulation
FSK   Frequency shift keying
FTP   File transfer protocol

GSC   Group switching exchange

HD(X)   Half duplex
HDLC   High-level data link control
Hz   Hertz or cycles per second

IAn   International alphabet n
IEEE   Institute of Electrical and Electronics Engineers
IMP   Interface message processor
IPSS   International packet switched service
IRC   International record carrier
ISO   International Standards Organisation
ISDN   Integrated services digital network

KSR   Keyboard send/receive

LAN   Local area network
LAP   Link access protocol
LAP-B   Link access protocol type B
LSM   Local systems management

mA   Milliampere – one thousandth of an ampere
Modem   Modulator-demodulator
MPX   Multiplex
MTBF   Mean time between failure
MTTR   Mean time to repair
MUX   Multiplexor

NAK   Negative acknowledgement
NAU   Network addressable unit
NCP   Network control program
NMM   Network measurement machine
NOS   Network operating system
NSP   Network services protocol
NTU   Network termination unit
NUI   Network user identification

OCE   Open communications environment
OSI   Open systems interconnection

pF   Picafarad – one billionth of a Farad
PABX   Private automatic branch exchange
PAD   Packet assembly/disassembly
PAM   Pulse amplitude modulation
PCM   Pulse code modulation
PDM   Pulse duration modulation
PDN   Public data network
PM   Phase modulation
PSE   Packet switching exchange
PSK   Phase shift keying
PSN   Public switched network
PSS   Packet switching service
PSTN   Public switched telephone network
PTT   Post, telegraph and telephone administration
PWM   Pulse width modulation

QAM   Quadrature amplitude modulation

RSEXEC   Resource sharing executive
RTS   Request to send
RTT   Regie des Telegraphes et des Telephones

SAP   Service access point
SDLC   Synchronous data link control
SDM   Synchronous division multiplexing
S/N   Signal to noise ratio
SNA   Systems network architecture
SOH   Start of header
SOM   Start of message
SSCP   System services control point
STX   Start of text
SYN   Synchronous idle

TDM   Time division multiplexing
TIP   Terminal interface message processor
TWX   Teletypewriter exchange service

VAN   Value added network
VTP   Virtual terminal protocol

WAN   Wide area network

Glossary of Technical Terms

Ampere: A unit of electric current flow.

Amplitude: The strength of a pulse or signal.

American Standard Code Information Interchange (ASCII): A seven bit code commonly used for data communications. The full code has 128 characters, including upper and lower case letters, digits, symbols and control characters. Details can be found in documents ISO7 or ISO646.

Asymmetric full-duplex: A full duplex circuit with a high speed message channel and a slower speed supervisory channel. It carries messages in both directions. The message channel carries the bulk of message data and the supervisory channel carries acknowledgements, repetition requests, etc., in the opposite direction. The direction of both reverse to effect communication in the opposite direction. This type of organisation eliminates the modem turnaround time inherent in sending both user data and supervisory messages on the same channel. Typically the message channel is 1200 bps and the supervisory channel is 75 bps.

Asynchronous transmission: Transmission in which there can be variable time intervals between characters with the bits of each character sent synchronously (at fixed intervals). A common method is to use start and stop bits to 'frame' a character when this is the case. Asynchronous transmission is also called start–stop transmission.

Baseband: The transmission of unmodulated signals usually by direct current and over short distances on a communications channel.

Baud: The standard unit for expressing the data transmission capability of lines, terminals and interface equipment. It equals the number of data significant line transitions (change in voltage of frequency) per second.

Baudot code: A five level code which was formerly the European standard for telegraph. Though supplanted in many instances by ASCII, it is still used for teletypewriter equipment.

BCC: *See* Block character check.

Binary synchronous communications (BI-SYNC): (Occasionally abbreviated to BSC) A method whereby synchronisation between a sending and receiving station is established before a message is sent and is checked and adjusted during transmission. The bits constituting characters are transmitted in a continuous stream and are separated by the receiving hardware using the synchronous information. It is a common method in medium and high speed data communications.

BISYN: See binary synchronous communications.

Bits per second (BPS): The number of binary digits transmitted per second in data communications.

Block character check (BCC): A final character of a block of a message which is constructed in accordance with an algorithm to assist in detecting errors.

Boolean function: A function which processes one or more inputs and produces a 'Yes' or 'No' answer.

Breakout box: A unit which can be placed in a circuit (say between a computer and a modem) to provide terminal connections for testing purposes.

Bridge: In networks, a bridge connects two homogeneous networks together to make possible communications between them.

Broadband: (Also called Wideband) A portion of a frequency spectrum which can be subdivided for some purpose (e.g. for use as several discrete channels).

Broadcast contention techniques: A technique of operating a small data network or multi-terminal data station in which a terminal with a message to send contends a transfer on the shared channel. *See also* Time slot allocation.

Bus network: (Also Highway network) A local area network topology organised around the use of a single major path for data transmission, e.g. Ethernet or Cheapernet using a coaxial cable as a bus.

Bus packet sharing technique: A packet technique for bus type networks in which a message is divided into packets of information which are transmitted individually; each packet provides headers and trailers for routeing and error detection.

Call collision: In systems where clear connections are established (by means of a call) prior to the exchange of information; the inability to complete the call due to causes such as 'receiver engaged'.

Capacitance: The ability of a circuit to store electrical charge. Undesirable in signalling lines because it tends to even out digital signalling levels.

Carrier: (Also Carrier wave) A wave generated by an oscillator and transmitted on a communications channel. It is modulated to carry data (for speech).

Carrier sense multiple access (CSMA): A contention method of operating a network whereby multiple nodes 'listen to' (sense) the communications medium and transmit when the medium is free from transmissions (silent). Note that propagation delay means that a node may sense silence in the short period before a message already on the medium reaches it, thus leading to collisions.

Carrier sense multiple access with collision avoidance (CSMA/CA): A CSMA method which incorporates an alternation between contention techniques and (in the event of a collision occurring) allocations of time slots. It reverts to contention when no allocated time slot has been used.

Carrier sense multiple access with collision detection (CSMA/CD): A CSMA technique in which, when a collision occurs, all nodes stop sending and then try again after the lapse of some time. Each node monitors its transmission constantly and compares the sensed transmission with what was originally sent. Any deviation indicates that a collision has occurred.

Carrier wave: *See* Carrier.

Chip: Slang word for a large scale integrated circuit.

Collision: The interference in transmission caused by more than one message appearing on the transmission medium at one time.

Collision presence pair in Ethernet: A pair of wires used by the transceiver to indicate the presence of multiple transmission on the coaxial cable bus.

Collision window time: The time it takes a message to travel the entire transmission medium in a contention type network; it is during this time that nodes may sense silence on the medium because the message has not yet reached them and thus may attempt to transmit.

Column parity bit: *See* Longitudinal parity bit.

Computer hardware: The physical components of a computer.

Computer software: The written instructions and programs relating to a computer.

Constant: A predetermined number that represents a fixed relationship having some significance in a calculation.

Control character: In any character set, characters whose function is the control of peripheral devices, e.g. printers.

Cyclic redundancy check: The use of a remainder when the entire bit stream is treated as a number and modulo divided by a constant as an error detection method.

Data bus: (Also Data highway) A major path for data transfer within a computer. By extension a major path for data transfer in a local area network where broadcasting is the transmission technique used.

Data circuit terminating equipment (DCE): A functional unit in a data communications system that performs some or all of the line interfacing functions such as signal conversion and synchronisation between a unit of data terminal equipment (DTE) and a data transmission line.

Data encapsulation: The process of enclosing data for transmission within additional routeing, error detection and correction data, as in encapsulating message data in a frame.

Data rate: *See* Data signalling rate.

Data signalling rate: (Also Bit rate) The rate in bits per second at which data is sent on in a communications channel.

Data terminal equipment (DTE): A functional unit in data communications that can imitate or receive (or both) messages; normally this is a computer or a terminal.

Data transfer: Movement of data within a computer system which does not make use of a communications link. When use is made of a communications link, the correct term is data transmission.

Delimit: To establish bounds to identify the beginning or end of a group or unit (as in 'delimit characters within a frame').

Demodulate To recover the original information from a modulated carrier wave – opposite of modulate.

Demodulation: The act of demodulating.

Deterministic: The ability of a network to guarantee that traffic will be delivered at the first attempt.

EBCDIC: (Usually pronounced ebb-sea-dick) *See* Extended binary code decimal interchange code.

Echo distortion: Distortion of a signal caused by elements of that signal being reflected back from an impedance change in the conductors, for example from the ends of an unterminated cable.

Empty time slot: A method of using a ring network where one or more empty packets circulate around the ring and a terminal wanting to transmit must wait for the arrival of such an empty packet.

Even parity: In parity checking error detection schemes using the parity bit to make certain each octet contains an even number of logic 1 bits.

Extended binary coded decimal interchange code (EBCDIC): An eight bit internal storage code used by IBM (and several other manufacturers) which is sometimes used in an IBM network for data transmission.

Farad: Unit of capacitance. A circuit has a capacitance of 1 Farad if it can store a coulomb (quantity of electrons) with a voltage rise of 1 volt.

Flow control: The method for controlling the movement of data for messages between two points as in a stream or sequence.

Forward error correction: A recovery procedure in which the receiving hardware analyses bit patterns and corrects small errors without requiring retransmission of the block containing the errors. *See* Hamming code.

Frame: (1) A pair of delimiters (e.g. start and stop bits) used for identifying the data between them. (2) In packet switching, HDLC and SDLC the unit of data transmission, beginning and ending with a flag.

Frame transmission: The transmission of an entire frame.

Frequency bandwidth: The lowest to the highest frequency used as a transmission medium. *See* Broadband.

Frequency distortion: The annoying or error causing change in frequency during data transmission.

Frequency shift keying: A signalling system using tones to represent digital levels.

Fully interconnected network: A local area network topology in which each unit is directly connected to every other unit.

Gateway: An interface between two networks in which a message passing from one to the other is 'wrapped' in the protocol of the destinaton network.

Graphic character: Non-alphanumeric character.

Guard band: A band of unused frequencies often about 500 Hz wide used to separate adjacent data bands in a frequency division multiplexed system.

Half duplex: (Sometimes HD(x)) A circuit in which messages can be sent in either direction, but only in one direction at a time.

Hamming code: A forward error correction code capable of detecting and correcting single bit errors and of detecting but not correcting multiple-bit errors.

Handshake: The initial interchange between modems (or other devices) prior to sending messages. The establishment of a 'clear' connection.

High level data link control (HDLC): An ISO definition of a standard communications interface for the transfer of data to and from packet switched networks. With respect to data format, it is very similar to SDLC.

Highway: *See* Data bus.

Highway network: *See* Bus network.

Horizontal parity bit: *See* Transverse parity bit.

Idle state: A character or bit sent when no other messages are being sent. It provides verification that the link is functioning and may also provide synchronisation data.

Impedance: The electrical opposition (measured in ohms) to the flow of a varying electrical current.

Interface: Any boundary between systems or functional units with different characteristics; thus a point where data passing across the boundary requires conversion to a suitable form.

LAN: *See* Local area network.

Lateral parity bit: *See* Transverse parity bit.

Layer: In architectures the logical construction method which provides an interface between lower (i.e. more hardware oriented) and higher (i.e. more user oriented) entities. For example, a physical layer might be the hardware used while a data link layer may exist immediately 'above' this and pass data to the physical layer for transmission.

Least significant bit: In a bit group the bit farthest to the right (when written), the bit transmitted first. It is analogous to the number '5' in the decimal number 87635 which is the least significant digit.

Link management: (Also Link protocol) It controls the interchange of data on a data link. For example, determining the code to be used, the type of signals, the modulation method, etc.

Local area network (LAN): A data network implemented with direct links between terminals within a restricted geographical area (e.g. an office block, a factory site).

Longitudinal parity bit: In two co-ordinate parity checking, the parity bit attached to a column of bits where the parity check applies to a block rather than a character. *See also* Transverse parity bit.

Loop network: A local area network topology consisting of a closed loop connecting a primary (master loop monitor) station with secondary stations. In operation, the primary sends out a message to the first secondary station and so on around the loop until the primary receives it and sends out a new initiating message.

Manchester encoding: A method of encoding data for transmission in which the line transition (change in voltage) occurs in the middle of a bit period, with a high to low transition signalling a 1 bit and a low to high transition signalling a 0 bit.

Mark condition: *See* Idle state.

Mesh: A network topology with highly or fully interconnected nodes.

Message format: The format in which a message is sent which may include headers indicating sender and recipient, trailers with control or error-detection data, etc.

Message sense signalling: A technique whereby nodes on a network listen to the medium and wait until the medium is silent to transmit.

Modem: From MOdulator to DEModulator. A unit of a data communications system that modulates and demodulates a carrier wave in order to represent data on a circuit.

Modem delay time: The time between the presentation of a digital signal at the interface and the time when the modulated carrier appears on the output line; or at the receiving end the time between receipt of the modulated signal and the time when the digital signal is presented to the interface of the DTE.

Modem turnaround time: On a half duplex system, the time required for the modems to change from the condition where 'A' is transmitting and 'B' is receiving to the condition where 'A' receives and 'B' transmits.

Modulate: To change a carrier wave in a data significant way.

Modulation: The process of changing the carrier wave.

Monitor: In a ring network topology, the node charged with checking the operation of the ring and removing corrupted packets.

Multicast: A method of sending one message to several terminals simultaneously, usually by means of a multicast address, which indicates by its type that the intended 'recipient' is actually a group of terminals.

Network interconnection technique: The techniques used to connect separate networks together.

Network management system: The software designed to control the operation of a network. It often provides the interface which the user sees and interacts with.

Node: A terminal or interchange point in a network which has significance for data routeing.

Non-deterministic: The inability of a network to guarantee information delivery at the first attempt.

Non-persistent CSMA: A CSMA technique in which the nodes do not retry a transmission immediately after a collision has been detected.

Non-persistent unslotted CSMA: A non-persistent CSMA technique where the nodes do not retry a transmission immediately after a collision but remain 'free' to transmit at any time.

Octet: Eight contiguous bits considered as a unit. In data communications the term is used in preference to byte.

Odd parity: In parity checking schemes, using the parity bit to create a byte, octet or work in which there is an odd number of logic 1 bits.

Ohm: A unit of electrical resistance.

Open systems interconnection (OSI): A standard for interconnecting dissimilar (heterogeneous) networks. It consists of a seven layer architecture.

Overheads: Time and other resources devoted to system function rather than to 'work'. In data transmission systems, overheads consist of such things as headers and trailers, parity bits, start-stop bits, etc., as these are not an effective part of the data to be transmitted but are necessary to the functioning of the network.

Parallel transmission: The simultaneous transmission of the bits of a character.

Parity bit: A bit devoted to use as a check bit to determine whether an error has occurred.

Peripheral: A functional unit that initiates or receives data transfer or transmission.

Persistent CSMA: In the CSMA mode, the case where nodes immediately retry a transmission following a collision. Persistence is based on probability; 1 persistent means that a node will immediately retry; 0.1 persistent means that the node has a 1 in 10 probability of retrying immediately.

Phase shift modulation: A method of modulation in which data is transmitted as different amounts of change in phase of a carrier wave.

Polling: A method of operating a data network in which the central site DTE and modem send short 'polling' messages to remote data stations in rotation. The remote data stations recognise their address and respond to polling messages sent to them. The remote station may simply acknowledge the polling message or, if it has data to send, will send it.

Power pair: In Ethernet or Cheapernet, the pair of wires which provides power to the transceiver.

Pre-allocated time slot: A discrete period of time allocated to a node in order for it to transmit data if it has any.

Processing time: The time between a DTE receiving data and the time it initiates a response message.

Propagating delay: The time between a signal being put on a transmission medium and the time it reaches points on that medium.

Random signalling: A method for operating a network with low levels of activity, whereby nodes simply transmit whenever they have something to transmit.

Reaction time: The time it takes for a DTE to 'realise' that it has received data and to initiate an acknowledgement.

Receiver pair: In Ethernet or Cheapernet, the pair of wires which carry encoded data from the transceiver to the data decoder and carrier sense circuitry in the physical layer.

Relay: A connection between two heterogeneous (unlike) networks which translates the protocol of one into the protocol of the other in transmitting messages between them.

Repeater: A device installed at spaced intervals in a communications cable in order to regenerate the attenuated signals.

Ring topology: A local area network topology consisting of a one or two way transmission medium arranged in a circular fashion where the nodes are connected by means of repeaters. A common example is the Cambridge ring.

Row parity bit: *See* Transverse parity bit.

Serial transmission: A transmission method whereby one bit is sent at a time. The sequential and single channel transmission of bits.

Service access point (SAP): A service access point in layered network architectures, the logical interface between the entities in one layer and the entities in an adjacent layer.

Service access point: Common service points between layers in the OSI model.

Signal regeneration: The process of reforming a signal of correct characteristics and transmitting in response to the receipt of an attenuated or distorted incoming signal.

Signal repeater: *See* Signal regeneration.

Signal throughput efficiency: The ratio of message data to transmitted data expressed as a percentage.

Simplex: A term designating a circuit or method of working where data is transmitted in one predesigned direction only.

Slotted non-persistent CSMA: A CSMA technique in which packet transmission is allowed only at discrete time intervals, thereby reducing the likelihood of collision though not eliminating it.

Source error: An error in transmission caused by the sender.

Space condition: A continuous line condition which represents a space (logic 0) in data transmission. *See* Mark condition.

Star topology: A local area network topology in which all remote stations are connected directly to a central computer system.

Statistical time division multiplexing (STDM): A method of improving circuit utilisation by collecting statistics on circuit use and using these to dynamically adjust multiplexing to eliminate time slots allocated to otherwise inactive devices or to give more time slots to very active devices.

Symbol substitution: An error correction method which relies on the human recipient being able to reconstruct garbled symbols in a message given that message and the correct parts of it.

Synchronous data link control (SDLC): A discipline for managing binary synchronous data communications (bisync) using full- or half-duplex transmission. SDLC systems use the CCITT V24 interface. *See also* High-level data link control.

Synchronous transmission: A transmission method in which timing reference is essential to the correct interpretation of bit patterns.

Teleprinter: A keyboard printer with a serial interface intended for synchronous communications.

Terminal equipment reaction time: The time required for a DTE to react to an incoming transmission.

Throughput efficiency: The ratio of the time spent transmitting data to the total time required to send a block of data and receive acknowledgement expressed as a percentage.

Time division multiplexing: (Often abbreviated to TDM) A multiplexing method whereby a single channel is used for the transmission of data and is allocated in turn for a short period of time to each of several sending or receiving units.

Time slot allocation: In time division multiplexing the allocation of a brief discrete period to a sending or receiving unit. In some networks, a period given to each node in turn to allow it to transmit.

Token: In token passing a message circulated around the nodes which carries no data but which grants permission to the holder to transmit.

Token passing: A network organisation wherein each node in turn is passed a token which gives it permission to transmit.

Topology: A means of classifying networks according to the patterns made by the nodes and interconnections.

Transceiver: An interfacing device or circuit which can both transmit and receive.

Transmission error: An error which arises during the transmission of data. *See also* Source error.

Transmission medium: The medium across which data can be transmitted. This can be radio waves, microwaves, copper wire, coaxial cable or fibre optical cable.

Transmit pair: In Ethernet or Cheapernet the pair of wires which transmits data to the transceiver.

Transverse parity bit: In two co-ordinate parity checking the parity bit for each character.

Tree network: A network topology in which nodes are arranged in a hierarchical structure with 'branching' transmission lines.

Two co-ordinate parity check: A method of parity checking in which each character has a parity bit associated with it and in which characters are grouped in a block. The last character of the block consists of parity bits for the column of bits within the block. *See* Block character check.

WAN: *See* Wide area network.

Wide area network: A data communications network usually spread over a large geographical area and using public or intermediate carriers to effect transmission.

Wideband: *See* Broadband.

X_{on} signal: A signal terminating a transmission which also signals the breaking of the logical connection between sender and receiver.

X_{off} signal: A signal establishing a handshake between sender and receiver, establishing a logical connection during which data are transmitted between them.

APPENDIX C
List of CCITT V Recommendations

V1   Equivalence between binary notation symbols and the significant conditions of a two condition code.

V2   Power levels for data transmission over telephone lines.

V3   International alphabet no. 5 for transmission of data and messages.

V4   General structure of signals of International Alphabet no. 5 for data and message transmission over public telephone networks.

V5   Standardisation of data signalling rates for synchronous data transmission in the general switched telephone network.

V6   Standardisation of data signalling rates for synchronous data transmission on leased telephone type circuits.

V10   Electrical characteristics for unbalanced double-current interchange circuits for general use with integrated circuit equipment in the field of data communications.

V11   Electrical characteristics for balanced double-current interchange circuits for general use with integrated circuit equipment in the field of data communications.

V13   Answer-back unit simulators.

V15   Use of acoustic coupling for data transmission.

V19   Modems for parallel data transmission using telephone signalling frequencies.

V20   Parallel data transmission modems standardised for universal use in the general switched telephone network.

V21   200 baud modem standardised for use in the general switched telephone network.

V22   1200 bps duplex modem standardised for use on the general switched telephone network.

V23   600/1200 baud modem standardised for use in the general switched telephone network.

V24   List of definitions for interchange circuits between data terminal equipment and data circuit terminating equipment.

V25   Automatic calling and/or answering on the general switched telephone network, including disabling of echo suppressors on manually established calls.

V26   2400 bps modem standardised for use on four wire leased circuits.

V26bis 2400/1200 bps modem standardised for use in the general switched telephone network.

V27 4800 bps modem standardised for use on leased circuits.

V27bis 4800 bps modem with automatic equaliser standardised for use on leased circuits.

V27ter 4800/2400 bps modem standardised for use in the general switched telephone network.

V28 Electrical characteristics for unbalanced double-current interchange circuits.

V29 9600 bps modem for use on leased circuits.

V30 Parallel data transmission systems for universal use on the general switched telephone network.

V31 Electrical characteristics for single-current interchange circuits controlled by contact closure.

V35 Data transmission at 48 kbps using 60 to 108 kHz group band circuits.

V36 Modems for synchronous data transmission using 60 to 108 kHz group band circuits.

V37 Synchronous data transmission at a data signalling rate higher than 72 kbps using 60 to 108 kHz group band circuits.

V40 Error indication with electromechanical equipment.

V41 Code independent error control system.

V50 Standard limits for transmission quality of data transmission.

V51 Organisation of the maintenance of international telephone-type circuits for data transmission.

V52 Characteristics of distortion and error rate measuring apparatus for data transmission.

V53 Limits for the maintenance of telephone-type loop circuits for data transmission.

V54 Loop test devices for modems.

V55 Specification for an impulsive noise measuring instrument for telephone-type circuits.

V56 Comparative tests of modems for use over telephone-type circuits.

V57 Comprehensive data test set for high data signalling rates.

APPENDIX D
List of CCITT X Recommendations

X1   International user classes of service in public data networks.

X2   International user facilities in public data networks.

X3   Packet assembly/disassembly facility (PAD) in a public data network.

X4   General structure of signals of International Alphabet no. 5 code for data transmission over public data networks.

X20   Interface between data terminal equipment (DTE) and data circuit terminating equipment (DCE) for start-stop transmission services on public data networks.

X20bis   V21-compatible interface between data terminal equipment (DTE) and data circuit terminating equipment (DCE) for start-stop transmission services on public data networks.

X21   General purpose interface between data terminal equipment (DTE) and data circuit equipment (DCE) for synchronous operation on public data networks.

X21bis   Use on public data networks of data terminal equipment which is designed for interfacing to synchronous V series modems.

X22   Multiplex DTE/DCE interface for user classes 3–6.

X24   List of definitions of interchange circuits between data terminal equipment and data circuit terminating equipment on public data networks.

X25   Interface between data terminal equipment (DTE) and data circuit terminating equipment (DCE) for terminals operating in the packet mode on public data networks.

X26   Electrical characteristics for unbalance double-current interchange circuits for general use with integrated circuit equipment in the field of data communications.

X27   Electrical characteristics for balanced double-current interchange circuits for general use with integrated circuit equipment in the field of data communications.

X28   DTE/DCE interface for a start-stop mode data terminal equipment accessing the packet assembly/disassembly facility (PAD) on a public data network situated in the same country.

X29   Procedures for the exchange of control information and user data between a packet mode DTE and a packet assembly/disassembly facility (PAD).

X30 Standardisation of basic mode page-printing machine in accordance with International Alphabet no. 5.

X31 Characteristics, from the transmission point of view, at the interchange point between data terminal equipment and data circuit terminating equipment when a 200 baud start-stop data terminal in accordance with International Alphabet no. 5 is used.

X32 Answer-back units for 200 baud start-stop machines in accordance with International Alphabet no. 5.

X33 Standardisation of an international text for the measurement of the margin of start-stop machines in accordance with International Alphabet no. 5.

X40 Standardisation of frequency shift modulated transmission systems for the provision of telegraph and data channels by frequency division of a primary group.

X50 Fundamental parameters of a multiplexing scheme for the international interface between synchronous data networks.

X50bis Fundamental parameters of a 48 kbps user data signalling rate transmission scheme for the international interface between synchronous data networks.

X51 Fundamental parameters of a multiplexing scheme for the international interface between synchronous data networks using a 10 bit envelope structure.

X51bis Fundamental parameters of a 48 kbps user data signalling rate transmission scheme for the international interface between synchronous networks using 10 bit envelope structure.

X52 Method of encoding anisochronous signals into a synchronous user bearer.

X53 Numbering of channels on international multiplex links at 64 kbps.

X54 Allocation of channels on international multiplex links at 64 kbps.

X60 Common channel signalling for synchronous data applications – data user part.

X61 Signalling system no. 7 – data user part.

X70 Terminal and transit control signalling system for start-stop services on international circuits between anisochronous data networks.

X71 Decentralised terminal and transit control signalling system on international circuits between synchronous data networks.

X75 Terminal and transit call control procedures and data transfer system on international circuits between packet switched data networks.

X80 Interworking of interchange signalling systems for circuit switched data services.

X87 Principles and procedures for realisation of international user facilities and network utilities in public data networks.

X92 Hypothetical reference connections for public synchronous data networks.

X93 Hypothetical reference connection for packet switched data transmission services.

X95   Network parameters in public data networks.

X96   Call progress signals in public data networks.

X110   Routeing principle for international public data service through switched public data networks of the same type.

X121   International numbering plan for public data networks.

X130   Provisional objectives for call set-up and clear-down times in public synchronous data networks.

X132   Provisional objectives for grade of service in international data communications over circuit switched public data networks.

X150   DTE and DCE test loops for public data networks in the case of X21 and X21bis interface.

X180   Administrative arrangements for international closed user groups (CUG).

X200   OSI reference model for CCITT applications.

APPENDIX E
List of Reference Books

(1) Gee, K. C. E. (1982) *Local Area Networks*. National Computing Centre Ltd. ISBN 0–85012–365–8.
(2) Housely, Trevor (1979) *Data Communications and Teleprocessing Systems*. Prentice-Hall. ISBN 0–13–197368–1.
(3) Green, Paul E. *ed.* (1982) *Computer Network Architectures and Protocols*. Plenum Press. ISBN 0–306–40788–4.
(4) Cheong, V. E. and Hirschheim, R. A. (1983) *Local Area Networks (Issues, Products and Developments)*. John Wiley & Sons. ISBN 471–90134–2.
(5) Xerox Ltd (1982) *The Ethernet (A Local Area Network) Version 2.0*.
(6) Tannebaum, Andrew S. (1981) *Computer Networks*. Prentice-Hall. ISBN 0–13–1646990.
(7) Scott, P. R. D. (1980) *Modems in Data Communications*. National Computing Centre Ltd. ISBN 0–85012–243–0.
(8) Deasington, R. J. (1985) *X25 Explained*. Ellis Horwood, Chichester, England. ISBN 0–85312–626–7.

APPENDIX F
List of Technical Papers and Magazine Articles

(1) Peatfield, Tony (1986) 'BP's Ethernet LAN'. *Communications Magazine*, **3**, no. 1.
(2) *Communications Magazine*, **2**, no. 10, October 1985, special issue on local area networks and IBM systems communications.
(3) *IEE Digest*, 1984, IEE Colloquium, 'Local area networks – how computers talk to each other', 10 May 1984.
(4) *IEEE Proceedings*, December 1983, special issue, 'Open systems interconnection (OSI) – new international standards architecture and protocols for distributed information systems.
(5) *Data Communications Magazine*, December 1981, special issue, 'Local area networks'.
(6) Shoch, J. F. and Hupp, J. A. 'Measured performance of an Ethernet local network', presented at Local Area Network Communications Network Symposium, Boston, May 1979.
(7) Crane, R. C. and Taft, E. A. 'Practical considerations in Ethernet local network', presented at Local Area Communications Network Symposium, Boston, May 1979.
(8) Bittel, R. (1977) 'On frame check sequence (FCS) generation and checking. *ANSI Working Paper X3-S34-7743*.
(9) Metcalfe, R. M. and Boggs, D. R. (1976) 'Ethernet: distributed packet switching for local computer networks'. *Communications of the ACM*, **19**, no. 7.
(10) Hammond, J. L., Brown, J. E. and Liu, S. S. (1975) Development of a transmission error model and an error control model. *Technical Report RADC-TR-75-138*, Rome Air Development Center.

Index